Twayne's English Authors Series

Sylvia E. Bowman, *Editor*

INDIANA UNIVERSITY

George Gascoigne

George Gascoigne

By RONALD C. JOHNSON

University of British Columbia

Twayne Publishers, Inc.   ::   New York

Preface

Of all the writers of the sixteenth century, George Gascoigne, despite his most important historical position, is perhaps the least understood and is certainly the most underrated. This statement may seem puzzling at first, for he is well known to modern critics of all literary genres—poetry, prose fiction, satire, drama, and criticism. Yet, very few critics speak of Gascoigne's creative ability; the extent of their interest is to define his niche in literary history. Those who do take the trouble to evaluate his work nearly always condemn it as second rate, as dull, or as being the first to "brake the ice for our quainter poets, who now write, that they may more safely swim through the main ocean of sweet poesy." This statement, made by R. T. Gent in 1615, is the main favorable critical approach taken to Gascoigne's work from shortly after his death to the present; and it serves, better than any other, to show why Gascoigne is seldom discussed as a "poet": his historical position is so important that it discourages a critical reading of his work.

The purpose of this book, therefore, is to discuss—as a critic, not as a historian—the writings of Gascoigne and to determine the merits and faults as they actually appear in the individual pieces, not as they appear in comparison to other writers or to poetical traditions which do not apply to him. Because Gascoigne considered himself primarily a poet and wrote more poetry than anything else, this book deals mainly with his poetry. His other literary writings are either experiments, translations, or single endeavors. In order to make fair, critical comments, I have had to examine the Petrarchan poetical concepts so popular with today's sixteenth-century critics and show their inappropriateness, to a large extent, as a method of judging Gascoigne's poetry and to see his position and achievements clearly. Also, Gascoigne's poetry and much of his prose is quite autobiographical; therefore, I found it necessary to repeat aspects of his life in sections other than the one dealing with his biography

Preface

so that the depth of his feeling or the accuracy of his satire
may be better understood.

Gascoigne is a highly interesting writer. He wrote lyric,
narrative, and satiric poetry; he wrote one of the earliest critical
treatises on poetry in the English language; he wrote one of
the first English novels; he first translated Italian comedy; and
was the first to use prose in the drama. His prose account of
the sack of Antwerp is one of the most vivid and realistic
descriptions of war in the English language. Yet he died feeling
that his life was a failure and that he had not accomplished all
that he felt to be in him. His work is important in that it records
the troubles and changes of his time, but also it vividly portrays
a sensitive human being struggling to understand the faults
and errors and evils he sees in that society and in himself.

RONALD CONANT JOHNSON

University of British Columbia

Contents

A Note on the Texts

The sources for all the Gascoigne quotations in this book are from the editions in the University of Illinois Library. They are the 1573 edition of *A Hundreth Sundrie Flowres,* the 1575 editions of *The Posies* and *The Glasse of Governement,* and the 1576 editions of *The Complaynt of Phylomene* and *The Steele Glas.* For the convenience of my readers, I have put after each quotation the page number where each can be found in the standard works by C. T. Prouty and J. W. Cunliffe. The note (Prouty, 175), for example, refers to C. T. Prouty, "George Gascoigne's *A Hundreth Sundry Flowres,*" *The University of Missouri Studies,* XVII, No. 2 (1942), p. 175. The note (Cunliffe, II, 79) refers to J. W. Cunliffe, *The Complete Works of George Gascoigne,* 2 vols. (Cambridge, 1910), vol. II, p. 79.

Chronology

c.1539   George Gascoigne born.

1555   Entered Gray's Inn to study and practice law.

1557   Entered Parliament as burgess for Bedford Borough.

1558   Attended coronation of Queen Elizabeth and left Gray's Inn for life at court.

1562   Married Elizabeth Bacon Bretton; fought with Edward Boyes and sent to prison.

1565   Returned to Gray's Inn to practice law.

1566   Produced *The Supposes* and *Jocasta*.

1568   Death of father and supposed disinheritance of George.

1570   Jailed for failure to pay debts.

1572(?)   Elected to Parliament as burgess for Midhurst.

1572   Volunteered for military service in the Dutch wars.

1573   Anonymous publication of *A Hundreth Sundrie Flowres*.

1574   Returned from soldiering on the Continent.

1575   Published *The Posies* and *The Glasse of Governement*; commissioned to write the entertainment for the Queen's Progress at Kenilworth.

1576   Published *The Steele Glas, The Complaint of Phylomene, The Droome of Doomes day, A Delicate Diet for daintie-mouthde Droonkardes, The Spoyle of Antwerpe,* and *The Grief of Joye*.

1577   Died October 7, at house of his friend George Whetstone.

CHAPTER 1

Biography

THE life of any poet is difficult to capture in a single essay or in an entire book. But this statement is particularly true of a poet of the Renaissance, for he was a man more truly involved in all aspects of life than a poet of perhaps any other period. The Renaissance poet was the Renaissance man—sociologist, explorer, politician, courtier, soldier, scientist, moralist, and actor. He worked in all literary mediums, and the label "poet" meant to him what the label "man of letters" may mean to us—that he was a journalist, a critic, a playwright, a writer of fiction, an essayist, and, of course, a writer of poetry of all kinds. There was no special niche reserved for a poet; all modes of writing were open to him. In prose, he could choose between the highly figured and self-conscious euphuistic style demonstrated most popularly by John Lyly and the precise plain style of Ben Jonson. In the drama, he could vary his style between the newly popular declamatory blank verse of Seneca and the terse, witty, realistic dialogue again epitomized by Jonson. His poetry could follow any one of a number of styles—the Petrarchan, the Classical Latin, or the traditional English. Most literary men of the period attempted at one time or another all forms and styles.

George Gascoigne, the major poet of the period just preceding Edmund Spenser and the High Renaissance, attempted all of these literary forms, experimented with them, and also introduced new ones. Through his literary career several values dominated his work—his patriotism, his ambition, and his honesty. His desire for social success and literary fame led him into all the forms of literary activity, the least result of which was a considerable addition to the developing forms of English expression. His patriotism led him to concentrate on the Anglo-Saxon facet of the English language and on earlier English models, most notably on Chaucer; this patriotism, combined with the honesty with which he approached his subjects, created a unique

13

bridge by which the native English strain of poetry, begun early in the Old English period, finding expression in Chaucer, and reaching the modern period through Thomas Wyatt, could leap the chasm created by Petrarch and the French and Latin poets to once again fit the pen of a master, John Donne. To some extent, Gascoigne created this bridge consciously, for he mentions many times the necessity of writing "like an Englishman." But his writings grew mainly from his experiences, and he found that the most effective way to communicate them was not in the Petrarchan style or in the decorated French style but in the English idiom which was bare of decoration but which emphasized not only metaphor but its poetic opposite—direct statement. An examination of his poetic technique occupies the major portion of this book, because poetry was Gascoigne's favorite artistic medium; but his important work in prose fiction, criticism, and drama are also discussed in depth, for they, too, are creative and intellectual achievements and give us additional means to apprehend the character and quality of the man.

Gascoigne was born sometime around 1539 of a well-to-do landowner and was reared to the life of a country gentleman.[1] However, his father was an argumentative man who had many quarrels with his neighbors, and young George, as he grew up, became involved with him in land and revenue disputes, even attending the law courts with his father. These early experiences apparently decided young George upon the law, for in 1555 he entered Gray's Inn to prepare for such a career. How successfully his studies progressed we do not know; more important is the fact that he made several strong friends who encouraged his literary talents and aided in the early productions of his plays.

In 1558 an event occurred which changed Gascoigne's life: the coronation of Queen Elizabeth. George attended in an official capacity in place of his ill father, and he was dazzled by what he saw at court. He left Gray's Inn and devoted all his time and money to set himself up as a courtier, hoping ultimately to gain recognition there and, subsequently, a position. However, as his funds diminished, he discovered that such quick fortune came only to a few, and his increasing debts forced him to go to the country to find a means of settlement. His time spent at court served, however, to awaken him to the vanity of such aspirations, and this newly found wisdom finds expression in many of his poems, such as that on the theme *Sat cito, si sat bene.*

During his time at court, Gascoigne met Elizabeth Bacon Bretton, a widow and possessor of some property; and he married her in 1561. The marriage brought considerable trouble to the couple, however, for Elizabeth apparently had earlier married Edward Boyes and then, believing the marriage to be illegal, married George. Boyes brought suit against them, took over some of Elizabeth's property, and had George and Elizabeth separated for a time before the court finally issued an injunction ending the suit. Besides the trouble with Boyes, Elizabeth and George were involved in a number of other legal disputes relative to disposition of property and inheritances, the substances of which are too complex to be reviewed here. The couple then left London and sought refuge in the country, but more legal difficulties beset them; and George finally decided to return to Gray's Inn, about 1565, to continue study of the law. Still unable to avoid legal problems, George again returned to the country, this time to take up farming, a part of his life recorded in the poem "The Complaint of the green knight." But trouble continued to follow him. After several escapades, such as the apparent stealing of his sheep by his mother and a deathbed disinheritance by his father (which had more drama than substance to it), Gascoigne, by 1571, was a ruined man. His creditors were pressing him for payment; he had little influence at court; and his youthful escapades before his marriage and his continual trouble after it had given him an unsavory reputation in the eyes of the church, the court, and the business community.

The substance of his writing reflects his experiences during this time. His early poetry follows the Petrarchan mode, as was fashionable for a courtier trying to attract attention to himself; and his novel investigates the game of courtly love as he saw it practiced at court. As his problems mounted, he became increasingly bitter, and this bitterness appears in his satires of the court and of society in general. Yet Gascoigne was sufficiently a craftsman to experiment with the forms he used. During his second stay at Gray's Inn he brought forth a new dramatic technique—the use of prose dialogue—and he helped produce the first Greek tragedy to be seen in England. His poetry experimented widely with Petrarchan forms and finally satirized the form itself; and he developed and refined verse forms, coining the term "poulter's measure" for one of them. His novel attempts to vary the standard prose fiction of the *novella* by using poems to record the emotional progress of the hero. So, during even this period of unrest, Gascoigne was still consciously an artist.

By 1571, Gascoigne had to find a way to meet his debts and to regain favor at court. The rising conflict between the Spanish and the Dutch gave him an opportunity to try a new career—soldiering. He went to the Dutch wars to fight for the Prince of Orange with a company of English volunteers. During the following four years, except for a brief interruption when he returned to England for a few months in 1572 to begin the publication of *A Hundreth Sundrie Flowres*, Gascoigne proved his worth as a soldier and as a leader of men; but he did not achieve the increase in fortune that he had desired. What did occur, and of immensely more value for us, was that he lost all illusions about warfare; as a result, he discovered and reported the falseness of allies, the treachery and cowardice of leaders, and the cruelty and uselessness of warfare generally. In a period when poets and statesmen glorified war and national ambitions, Gascoigne struck at both. In *The Steele Glas* he satirized greedy princes, and in "Dulce Bellum Inexpertis" he exposed the life of a soldier for what it really is. He was disillusioned by his superiors; he was discouraged by his failure to profit from his fighting, even losing much of his earned pay because of a trumped-up charge of treason, and spending the last few months before his return to England in imprisonment. But on his return to England his fortunes rose, and the direction of his career changed.

When Gascoigne returned to England from Holland in 1574, he was met by the furor caused by publication of his *A Hundreth Sundrie Flowres*. The copies of it had been confiscated, and Gascoigne was accused of libel and immorality. His first task was to change his bad reputation, and he immediately revised the *Flowres* into *The Posies* of 1575. He removed much of the objectionable material, but even this edition was partially confiscated. Next, he set about revising his popular image, which he accomplished through prefatory letters to his works, such as the "Epistle to the reverend Divines," and by writing morally didactic pieces such as *The Droome of Doomes Day*, *A Delicate Diet for daintiemouthde Droonkardes*, *The Grief of Joye*, and the play *The Glasse of Governement*. By 1576 his career was in the ascendance: he had a wealthy patron; his writings were widely read and well received at court; and he had succeeded in gaining a position at court as an agent for William Cecil, Elizabeth's chief minister, to report on affairs on the Continent, a post which allowed him to write *The Spoyle of Antwerpe.*

But in 1577, Gascoigne was struck by an illness which he could not overcome. He languished some months at the home of an old friend and poet, George Whetstone, and then died in October, 1577. The irony was complete: as Fortune's Wheel was at last lifting him to the top and within reach of the worldly success that he had sought for so long, the man himself was not able to grasp the offering.

CHAPTER 2

Gascoigne and Petrarch

BEFORE we begin the examination of Gascoigne's poetry, we must first lay the ghost of Petrarchan criticism. Too often, Gascoigne has been seen only in relation to a school of poetry to which he did not subscribe, and the resulting attitude toward him has been unjust. The Petrarchan school of poetry was by far the most influential during the last half of the century and accounted for the majority of all poetry written. There were other influences: the poetry of Ovid, the French Troubadors, the medieval Latin poets, Chaucer, and many others; therefore a Petrarchan metaphor which exemplifies to one critic the transiency of life may justly be considered a condensation of a medieval allegory of death by another. The boundaries between poetical influences are indistinct, but within such boundaries, certain tendencies can be found which more evidently point to one source than another; and the poems of Petrarch are the clearest and most popular of all the poetic influences in the second half of the century.

In many ways for sixteenth-century England, Petrarch signaled the change from the spirituality of the Middle Ages toward the robust, earthy paganism of the Renaissance.[1] In mood and tone, he varies between reverence and sensuousness; in content, he uses fewer metaphysical subtleties in his poetry than do the medieval poets, but he employs more mythological allusions and illustrations. His treatment of women, though always in the courtly tradition, is often sensuous. His usually sympathetic and effective references to nature are far from the stylized treatment given it by his predecessors. We need only compare the earl of Surrey's "The Soote Season" sonnet with John Barclay's "Certain Eglogues" to see the great distance between sixteenth-century poets before and after the introduction of Petrarch. Because Petrarch's love poems were most often copied and imitated, this chapter investigates mainly the relationships between Petrarch and Gascoigne in their love poetry.

There can be no doubt that Petrarch greatly influenced Gascoigne. In the dedication to "The Grief of Joye" one of his major poems, Gascoigne admits Petrarch as his model: "Towching the *Methode* and *Invention,* even as *Petrark* in his workes *De remediis utriusque fortunae,* dothe recoupt the uncerteine Joyes of men in severall dialogues, so have I in thes *Elegies* distributed the same into sundrie songes" (Cunliffe, II, 514). Gascoigne then voices his debt to Petrarch in the poem itself; but he makes an important addition:

> But as the man, whiche serves his prentishoode,
> With Artisanes. . . .
> . . . I venter my good will
> Yn barreyne verse, to doe the best I can,
> Like *Chaucers* boye, and *Petrarks* jorneyman.
> (Cunliffe, II, 517)

Further on he says again:

> But if some English woorde, herein seme sweet,
> Let *Chaucers* name, exalted be therefore,
> Yf any verse, doe passe on plesant feet,
> The praise thereof, redownd to *Petrarks* lore.
> (Cunliffe, II, 518)

Gascoigne clearly considers Petrarch and Chaucer to be equally worthy of respect. At the same time, we realize that Gascoigne knows exactly what each poet has given him and what each is respected for: Chaucer, for an English flavor in diction; Petrarch, for smoothness and grace in verse. Gascoigne, who read Petrarch in the original Italian, recognized Petrarch's importance to English poets. But his own indebtedness to Petrarch is an illusory one which has, unfortunately, misled many critics. We need, therefore, to examine the influence of Petrarch on Gascoigne's prosody and on his subject matter.

I *The Sonnet*

The sonnet form is perhaps the greatest debt Gascoigne's prosody has to Petrarch, but whether he took it directly from Petrarch, or from Wyatt's and Surrey's use of it, is not certainly known. Wyatt first brought the Italian sonnet into English; of the more than thirty sonnets of his remaining to us, at least fifteen are direct translations from Petrarch, and seven are adaptations or paraphrases.[2] These sonnets are constructed of fourteen lines of iambic pentameter; the rhyme scheme is variable and not like the original; and the poem's theme is established in the octave and concluded in the sestet. His meter is quite rough, varying between a four- and a five-stressed line; and, for at least this reason, his sonnets are generally unsuccessful.[3] After Wyatt, Surrey experimented with the sonnet form; he developed what many call the "English" sonnet, which differs from the Italian sonnet by having a more variable rhyme scheme and, more importantly, by developing the theme of the sonnet in three quatrains instead of in an octave and a sestet and by summarizing the author's attitude in a rhyming couplet at the end.

Between Surry and Gascoigne, many sonnets were written by such men as Nicholas Grimald; but there was no further development of the form. Then, in 1575, Gascoigne published his *Posies*, which contains, along with a number of sonnets in both the Italian and the English form, his "Certayne notes of Instruction." In it, he defined a sonnet as being of "fourtene lynes, every line conteyning tenne syllables. The firste twelve do rhyme in staves of foure lines by crosse meetre, and the last twoo ryming togither do conclude the whole." He says nothing about the thematic development, but he does mention the use of the rhyming couplet, thus showing a break with the Italian original.

Of the three sonnet versifiers—Wyatt, Surrey, and Gascoigne—Gascoigne is the most regular in form, as might be expected since the sonnet was several decades old before he began working with it. Wyatt's are often rough in meter, variable in rhyme scheme, and sometimes fail to observe octave-sestet division in thought. Also, it seems, he chose the worst parts of Petrarch to translate. An example is his translation of Petrarch's "Sonnet in Life, XC," from *Sonnets and Songs*, which contains many of the oxymorons that later became highly popular with English poets:

> I fynde no peace and all my warr is done;
> I fere and hope, I burne and freise like yse;
> I fley above the wynde yet can I not arrise;
> And noght I have and all the worold I seson;
> That loseth nor locketh holdeth me in prison
> And holdeth me not, yet can I scape nowise;
> Nor letteth me lyve nor dye at my devise.

> And yet of deth it gyveth none occasion.
> Withoute Iyen, I se; and withoute tong I plain;
> I desire to perisshe, and yet I aske helthe;
> I love an othre, and thus I hate my self;
> I fede me in sorrowe and laughe in all my pain;
> Likewise displeaseth me boeth deth and lyffe;
> And my delite is causer of this stryff.[4]

In this sonnet, Wyatt rhymes the last two lines, but they do not function as a final couplet. Petrarch, of course, does not rhyme the last two lines of a sonnet.

After Wyatt, Surrey changed the sonnet form to that of the English sonnet. The couplet at the end is often an epigrammatic device that can be removed from the poem and enjoyed by itself; it is often not an essential part of the poem, as in the following adaptation from Petrarch's *Sonnets and Songs*, "Sonnet in Death," XLII:

> The soote season, that bud and blome furth bringes,
> with grene hath clad the hill and eke the vale;
> the nightingale with fethers new she singes;
> the turtle to her make hath tolde her tale;
> Somer is come, for every spray now springes;
> the hart hath hong his old hed on the pale;
> the buck in brake his Winter cote he flinges;
> the fishes flote with newe repaired scale;
> the adder all her sloughe awaye she slonges;
> the swift swalow pursueth the flyes smale;
> the busy bee her honye now she minges.
> Winter is worne, that was the flowers bale.
> And thus I see among these pleasant thinges
> eche care decayes, and yet my sorrow springes.[5]

In this sonnet, Surrey expands the eight-line description given to spring by Petrarch into twelve lines, and Surrey compresses into a final couplet the vivid contrast of death-in-life which informs all the lines of Petrarch's original sonnet. Surrey's poem stands as a beautiful piece on spring, complete without the last two lines; the couplet is almost an intrusion.

The advantages of the Surrey sonnet form were readily seen, and such poets as Nicholas Grimald and uncertain authors in *Tottel's Miscellany* (1557) availed themselves of both forms. The sonnet by an "Uncertain Author," entitled "A Praise of Petrarke and of Laura his ladie," is a close adaptation of Petrarch both in organization and in rhyme scheme, except for the inevitable final rhyming couplet.[6] Nicholas Grimald's "Concerning Virgils Eneids," on the other hand, follows Surrey's sonnet form. Yet several others, such as Grimald's "An epitaph of Sir *James Wilford* Knight," have no form or thematic development whatever; and the lack of it perhaps accounts in some measure for their obscurity.

From Surrey to Gascoigne, no important change occurred in the sonnet. Gascoigne, however, became quite interested in the form and experimented with it. In several of his sonnets, he returns to the Italian style of octave-sestet theme development, but he retains the English rhyme scheme and ends with a rhyming couplet, as in the following:

> A HUNDRETH sonnes (in course but not in kind)
> Can witnesse well that I possesse no joye:
> The feare of death which fretteth in my mynd
> Consumes my hart with dread of darke anoye.
> And for eche sonne a thousand broken sleepes
> Devide my dreames with fresh recourse of cares:
> The youngest sister sharpe hir sheare she kepes,
> To cut my thred and thus my life it weares.
> Yet let such dayes, such thousand restlesse nightes,
> Spit forth their spite, let fates eke showe their force:
> Deathes daunting dart where so his buffets lights,
> Shall shape no change within my friendly corse:
> But dead or live, in heaven, in earth, in hell,
> I wilbe thine, where so my carkase dwell.
>
> (Prouty, 110-11)

The thought breakes in the ninth line, but the rhyme scheme is Surrey's. Gascoigne uses the Surrey sonnet form in an interesting exercise based upon the theme *Sat cito, si sat bene.* He links together seven sonnets, the first line of each succeeding sonnet being the last line of each preceding one, until he has fully developed the theme in question. An interesting experiment, it is not totally successful.

Gascoigne experimented briefly with the form of the sonnet as well as with its use. In "The introduction to the Psalme of De Profundis," he experiments successfully with the formal thematic development; he breaks the thought in the seventh line rather than in the eighth. To balance the effect, he also changes the rhyme scheme. The result is a sonnet that does not end in a rhyming couplet but which does come quite close to capturing Petrarch's own use of rhyme:

> The Skies gan scowle, orecast with mistie clowdes,
> When (as I rode alone by London way,
> Cloaklesse, unclad) thus did I sing and say:
> Behold, quoth I, bright *Titan* how he shroudes
> His dead abacke, and yelds the raine his reach,
> Till in his wrath *Dan Jove* have soust the soile,
> And washt me wretch, which in his travaile toile.
> But holla (here) doth rudenesse me apeach,
> Since *Jove* is Lord and king of mightie power,
> Which can commande the Sunne to shew his face,
> And (when him list) to give the raine his place.
> Why do not I my wery muses frame,
> (Although I be well soused in this shoure,)
> To wrighte some verse in honor of his name?
>
> (Prouty, 165)

With the exception of a few of Gascoigne's sonnets, the rhyming couplet seems to be the one ever-present addition to the sonnet form in England; but it is used differently by Surrey and Gascoigne. Surrey's couplet frequently can be removed from the poem without distorting the meaning, but Gascoigne's couplet is organic to the whole poem—the poem would not be complete without it. Wyatt's couplet functions in much the same manner as Gascoigne's.

Gascoigne, then, is directly influenced in one way by the introduction of Petrarch into English in that he writes many of his poems in the sonnet form. Fairly successful in its use, he handles it more smoothly than Wyatt but less spectacularly than Surrey. Whether Gascoigne would have used the sonnet if Wyatt and Surrey had not, is doubtful; for, although he was familiar with Petrarch in the original, his lyrical muse is much more in tune with *Tottel's Miscellany* than with voices from foreign lands. Yet, he remained patterned closely enough upon Petrarch to preserve the Italian organization of thought in several of his sonnets; and he occasionally reproduced Petrarch's rhyme scheme successfully—a feat seldom accomplished by his contemporaries.

II *The Content of Love*

Petrarch is of greater significance to the sixteenth century in a way other than in giving impetus to the sonnet form. In his

attitude toward women, in his concept of love, and in the cre-
ation of certain conceits, metaphors, and descriptive phrases,
he gave to the poets of the latter two-thirds of the century a
whole new subject to exploit—a task which they accomplished
with such energy that, by the end of the century, they had
exhausted it completely and had even begun to ridicule it. The
extensive use of these conventions comes close to defining a
whole school of poetry, the Petrarchan, as mentioned earlier.
I have set forth these characteristics in order to use the term
"Petrarchan" without confusion, and to aid us in determining
the extent of Gascoigne's reliance upon them and his deviation
from them. They are as follows:

1. The poet addresses a love poem to a lady who corresponds
    to Petrarch's Laura (but who sometimes is a real person).
2. The lady is often given a Classical name, such as Sidney's
    Stella, or Daniel's Delia.
3. The poet-lover presents himself as ardent and impetuous.
4. The poet praises his mistress' superlative beauty, using
    the description supplied by Petrarch: golden hair, roses
    in her cheeks, ruby lips, ivory breasts, and so forth.
5. The poet-lover dwells only on the misery of love, hence the
    appearance later of the conventional invocation to sleep
    to allay his pain.
6. The poet uses standard phrases which are seemingly self-
    contradictory, or oxymoronic, such as "I burn, I freeze."
7. The poet-lover always disclaims any credit for whatever
    merits his poetry may have, citing the inspiration of his
    mistress as the reason for the poem's merit.
8. The poet promises to protect the youth of his lady and the
    love of the poet against time by means of his poetry; this
    is the eternizing theme.

The sonnet by Wyatt which I quoted earlier, contains several of the usual oxymoronic phrases: peace-war, fear-hope,
burn-freeze. These phrases, and all the Petrarchan conventions,
abound in the poetry of the century after Wyatt introduced
them. The courtly poets, looking for fashionable ways to ad-
dress themselves to the ladies of the court, adapted Petrarch's
material to their own uses. The result was a heavy flow of poetry
in the Petrarchan style, most of it inferior to the original.

The series of poems addressed to Laura, collected in *The
Sonnets and Songs of Francis Petrarch*, are divided into two

sections—those written during her lifetime called "Sonnets in Life," and those written after her death, called "Sonnets in Death." Many characteristics of Petrarch's poetry found their way into Gascoigne's poetry, but many other characteristics did not, even though he wrote while Petrarch's influence was quite strong—at a time when the worst of the Petrarchan poetry was being written. If Gascoigne did not reject the Petrarchan style outright, he managed to shift the emphasis away from slavish compliment to the lady toward an ironical approach to the lover's position. Gascoigne's relationship to Petrarch is important because it shows to some extent that the mid-century poets —those between Wyatt and Spenser—were not turning mindlessly to Classical or foreign models, or sitting stagnant hoping for a Spenser to come along and propel them forward again. What they were doing was to take what was valuable from the influx of foreign verse and combine it with the older traditions of English poetry in an attempt to progress on two levels—the lyrical expressiveness of the more colloquial early English songs and ballads coupled with the smoother, more refined expression of the foreign models, of which Petrarch was the major one.

Petrarch's attitude in verse toward his Laura is one of his most widely copied characteristics. His poetry is quite sensual, yet there is something which elevates the person of Laura and removes her from the immediate caress of the lover. She becomes almost a goddess, forcing the lover-poet to express his love in ardent compliments, comparisons, and self-searchings, but seldom allowing him to demand her faithfulness or a return of love. Also, perhaps because Petrarch could never possess Laura, and perhaps because many of his poems were written about his love for her after her death, there is a distinct flavor of the hopelessness of unrequited passion, probably the reason that much of the century's borrowings were complaints of a lover to his mistress. The following sonnet by Petrarch blends, for example, several of the elements that were borrowed by the sixteenth century:

> That ever-cruel, ever-honoured day
> Laid so deep in my heart her image true,
> That neither style nor talent can convey
> What my memory often brings me to.
>
> The act adorned with pity's gentleness
> And the sweet bitter meaning that I heard,

Made one doubt whether woman or goddess
Cleared the air around us that had been blurred.

Fine gold the hair, warm snow the face appears,
Lashes of ebony, eyes like coupled stars
From where Love bent the bow that made our scars;

Pearls and vermilion roses where the hive
Of sorrow found a voice pure and alive;
Her sighs like flame, and like crystal her tears.[7]

This description of the Petrarchan mistress—gold hair, ebony
lashes, eyes like coupled stars, sighs like flame, tears of crystal—
is quite familiar to readers of sixteenth-century lyric poetry, and
the phrases "sweet-bitter," "ever-cruel, ever-honoured" exhibit
the type of oxymoron which the poets borrowed. Petrarch uses
much sensuous description, also, as when, in "Sonnet in Life,"
CXXVII, he says: "What miracle when she among the grass/
Sits like a flower, or when I see her brush/ With her white breast
the green of a small bush!"[8] And again, giving voice to his frustrations, he writes in "Sonnet in Life," CXXXI:

I watch, I burn, I weep, and she who tears
My heart is always here for my sweet grief;
War is my state, full of anger and cares,
And only in her thought I find relief.[9]

All these attitudes are commonplace in the love poetry of the
century: the lover attempting to win his mistress by means of
compliments and comparisons; expressing his passion by glowing,
often sensuous, descriptions; and expressing his distress and
recording his mental and physical conflicts.

When the sonnet was introduced into England, it was used
most often for matters of love; and English writers, such as
Nicholas Grimald and the poets of *Tottel's Miscellany,* tended
to retain in their poetry the attitudes established by Petrarch.
Gascoigne, however, changed the use of the sonnet somewhat;
for, as he says in his "Certayne notes of Instruction," "sonnets
serve as well in matters of love as of discourse." He uses the
sonnet to praise those with whom he has no romantic attach-
ment ("In Praise of Lady Zouche"); his "Introduction to ... De
Profundis" is almost a narrative piece and serves only to record
the occasion of the writing of the poem. The seven sonnets
based upon the theme *Sat cito, si sat bene* display cleverness

and some satire but no romantic theme. He uses the sonnet to praise a geographical location, as in "Not stately *Troye*," which sings the beauties of "Founteine belle eau." And again experimenting with the use of the sonnet, Gascoigne wrote a three-sonnet linked sequence telling his personal interpretation of the history of Lucius Apuleius; in this instance, the sonnets have a distinctly moralistic flavor. Thus, Gascoigne expanded the use of the sonnet beyond merely the carrying of a message of love.

Where Gascoigne does use the sonnet form to tell of his love, we notice a distinct difference in tone between his poems and Petrarch's. Petrarch is always refined, well mannered, and, if sensual, subtly so. In love poems other than sonnets Gascoigne sometimes approaches these characteristics; but he usually does not in his love sonnets, of which the following from *The Adventures of Master F. J.* is an example:

> That selfe same day, and of that day that hower,
> When she doth raigne, that mockt Vulcan the Smith:
> And thought it meete to harbor in hir bower,
> Some gallant gest for hir to dally with.
> That blessed hower, that blist and happie daye,
> I thought it meete, with hastie steppes to go
> Unto the lodge, wherein my Ladye laye,
> To laugh for joye, or ells to weepe for wo.
> And lo, my Lady of hir wonted grace
> First lent hir lippes to me (as for a kisse:)
> And after that hir body to embrace,
> Wherein dame nature wrought nothing amisse.
> What followed next, gesse you that knowe the trade,
> For in this sort, my Frydayes feast I made.
>
> (Prouty, 74)

This sonnet is characterized by bawdiness and coarseness in taste; yet it has wit and vigor and a pervading sense of male satisfaction which separates it as far from the meditative and melancholy sonnets of Petrarch as the use of related material permits.

Gascoigne, however, did not neglect the Petrarchan influence; familiar with the Petrarchan conventions, he used them often, as in the following:

> I laugh sometimes with little lust,
> So jest I oft and feele no joye:

> Myne ease is builded all on trust,
> And yit mistrust breedes myne anoye.
> I live and lack, I lack and have:
> I have and misse the thing I crave.
>   (Prouty, 127)

and:

> The straightest tree that growes upon one only roote:
> If that roote fayle, will quickly fade, no props can do it boote.
>
> I am that fading plant, which on thy grace did growe.
> Thy grace is gone, wherefore I mone, and wither all in woe.
>
> The tallest ship that sayles, if shee to Ancors trust:
> When ancors slip and cables breake, hir helpe lyes in the dust.
>
> I am the ship my selfe, myne Ancor was thy faith:
> Which now is fled, thy promise broke, and I am driven to death.
>   (Prouty, 128)

In the latter example, Gascoigne builds up conceit after conceit, using all the Petrarchan metaphors in their standard form; and he produces a poem composed of four-line pieces, but without any direction and with little cohesiveness. When Gascoigne enters the tradition, he does it with great enthusiasm. Yet, Gascoigne, as early as 1572, had gone far enough beyond his contemporaries to be able to criticize gently their use of the conventions, as he does in the following poem:

> I Smile sometimes although my griefe be great,
> To heare and see these lovers paint their paine,
> And how they can in pleasaunt rimes repeate,
> The passing pangs, which they in fancies faine.
> But if I had such skill to frame a verse,
> I could more paine than all their panges rehearse.
>
> Some say they find nor peace, nor power to fight,
> Which seemeth strange: but stranger is my state:
> I dwell in dole, yet sojorne with delight,
> Reposed in rest, yet weried with debate.
> For flatte repulse, might well apease my will,
> But fancie fights to trie my fortune still. . . .
>
> How live I then, which thus drawe foorth my daies?
> Or tell me how, I found this fever first?

What fits I feele? what distance? what delayes?
What grief? what ease? what like I best? what worse?
These things they tell, which seeke redresse of paine,
And so will I, although I coumpt it vaine. . . .

(Here follows four verses stating his disorders.)

Tormented thus without delaies I stand,
Alwaies in one and evermore shal be,
In greatest griefe when helpe is nearest hand,
And best at ease if death might make me free:
Delighting most in that which hurts my hart,
And hating change which might relieve my smart.

Yet you dere dame: to whome this cure perteines,
Devise betimes some drammes for my disease,
A noble name shall be your greatest gaines,
Whereof be sure, if you will worke mine ease.
And though fond fooles set forth their fitts as fast,
Yet grant with me that Gascoignes passion past.
                                        (Prouty, 147-48)

He ridicules the lover's complaints, the use of rhetorical questions, and the use of antithetical statements; however, this
ridicule suggests an ambiguity in the poem that enhances the
poet's mood quite well; for, to prove his own grief, he uses
these same devices, yet with a sense of hopelessness which
serves to emphasize their uselessness. He even suggests, as a bribe,
to put his lady's name in verse. Gascoigne often turns the
Petrarchan devices away from their conventional uses in order
to achieve this ironic effect.

Gascoigne rarely uses the standard terms of physical description which the century took from Petrarch; but, in one sonnet
in which he does, he employs them to his own ironic end and
produces a successful poem. In a sonnet to his mistress, part of
The Adventures of Master F. J., they work organically within
the poem to produce, not a standard compliment, but a complex,
completed thought:

The stately Dames of Rome their Pearles did weare,
About their neckes to beautifie their name:
But she (whom I doe serve) hir pearles doth beare,
Close in hir mouth, and smiling shewes the same.
No wonder then, though ev'ry word she speakes,
A Jewell seeme in judgment of the wise,

Since that her sugred tongue the passage breakes,
Betweene two rockes, bedekt with pearles of price.
Hir haire of golde, hir front of Ivory
(A bloudy hart within so white a brest)
Hir teeth of Pearle, lippes Rubie, christall eye,
Needes must I honour hir above the rest:
Since she is fourmed of none other moulde,
But Rubie, Christall, Ivory, Pearle, and Golde.

(Prouty, 77)

The precious stones and metals mentioned in the last line are all standard Petrarchan terms of description, ordinarily used strictly as compliments; but in Gascoigne's sonnet, they suggest hardness and coldness. Her jaws are two rocks; her front or breast, not her skin, is ivory. She has a crystal eye, hard and uncompromising; and she was formed in a mold excluding any softer material. Thus, we are given a portrait of a beautiful, cold woman; yet underneath the uncompromising exterior, and completely hidden by it, is a passionate heart, known to the poet only by intuition. For not even in her conversation does she betray any feelings. Her words are jewels, pearls of wisdom; but they are to be judged not by her lover but by wise men. The poet is telling his mistress that he admires her beauty, stands in awe of her mind, and is interested by the suggestion of hidden passion which contrasts so sharply with her appearance.

Gascoigne uses conventional Petrarchan oxymorons quite often in his poetry. There are many lines, such as "Amid my Bale I bath in blisse,/ I swim in heaven, I sinke in hell," from his "A straunge passion of another Author." He uses them to emphasize his mood, but to modern readers the device has lost its effect, and we allow Gascoigne very little success in using it.

In many of his love poems that are not sonnets, Gascoigne displays some similarity to Petrarch. The particular attitude in which the one poet most closely resembles the other is that of a half-sad, half-sweet reflection which contains within it elements of both lament and didacticism. We see this attitude in many of Petrarch's sonnets and songs in which he laments Laura's loss while displaying what she has taught him of life, as in "Sonnet in Death," CCXLVIII:

My lofty flame, more than the fairest fair,
That here had heaven as a courteous friend,

Before her time has reached her journey's end,
And returns to her land her star to share.

Now I begin to wake, I understand
That she for our own good fought my desire,
And made my youthful wishes to retire
Tempering them with a look hard and bland.

I thank her sour and her holy device
That with her face and her sweet anger's bolts
Bid me in burning think of my salvation.

O lovely arts bringing worthy results,
One working with the tongue, one with the eyes,
I for her glory, she for my vocation![10]

Although the material is different, the mood is quite the same
in these examples from Gascoigne:

I that my race of youthfull years had roon,
Always untyed, and not (but once) in thrall,
Even I which had the fieldes of freedome woon,
And liv'd at large, and playde with pleasurs ball:
Lo now at last am tane againe and taught,
To tast such sorowes, as I never sought.

I love, I love, alas I love indeede,
I crie alas, but no man pitties me:
My woundes are wyde, yet seeme they not to bleede,
And hidden woundes are hardly heald we see.
Such is my lucke to catch a sodeyne clappe
Of great mischaunce in seeking my good happe. . . .

Thus still I toyle, to till the barreyne land,
And grope for grapes among the bramble briers:
I strive to sayle and yet I sticke on sand,
I deeme to live, yet drowne in deep desires.
These lots of love are fitte for wanton will,
Which findes too much, yet must be seeking still.

(Prouty, 140-41)

and:

When I record within my musing mind,
The noble names of wightes bewicht in love:
Such sollace for my selfe therin I find,
As nothing may my fixed fansie move:

> But paciently I will endure my wo,
> Because I see the heavens ordayne it so. . . .
>
> So that to end my tale as I began,
> I see the good, the wise, the stoute, the bolde:
> The strongest champion and the learnedst man,
> Have bene and be, by lust of love controld.
> Which when I thinke, I hold me well content,
> To live in love, and never to repent.
>
> (Prouty, 141-42)

The strong element of didacticism can be seen particularly in the second example. With Gascoigne, what is lost is his youth; what has been gained is a rueful sort of wisdom. His poetry abounds with the expression of this particular mood, and he expresses it more poignantly and effectively than he does any other.

The other Petrarchan conventions have little influence over Gascoigne. Unless forced by the direction of a narrative situation, as in *F. J.*, he does not present a lover petitioning his mistress for attentions; nor does he always observe the rules of courtesy in his addresses. He is much more concerned with exhibiting himself—his complaints, his appearance, his prowess; and the text of the poem is often spoken directly to his mistress—her personality is part of the poem and her actions are rehearsed, commented upon, and enjoyed or despised by the poet, unlike Petrarch, who speaks about his mistress but seldom directly to her. Gascoigne says, in a farewell to his mistress:

> Thy byrth, thy beautie, nor thy brave attyre,
> (Disdainefull Dame, which doest me double wrong)
> Thy high estate, which sets thy hart on fire,
> Or new found choyce, which cannot serve thee long,
> Shall make me dread, with pen for to reherse
> Thy skittish deedes, in this my parting verse. . . .
>
> And though my mind, have small delight to vaunt,
> Yet must I vowe, my hart to thee was true:
> My hand was alwayes able for to daunt,
> Thy slandrous fooes, and kepe their tongues in mew.
> My head (though dull) was yet of such devise,
> As might have kept thy name alwayes in price. . . .
>
> And farre from thee now must I take my flight,
> Where tongues may tell, (and I not see) thy fall:

> Where I may drinke these draggs of thy despight,
> To purge my Melancholike mind with all.
> In secrete so, my stomacke will I sterve,
> Wishing thee better than thou doest deserve.
>
> (Prouty, 124-25)

In this poem, Gascoigne praises himself for his honorable actions but blames her for their separation. The poem is spoken to the woman directly and seemingly would have small value if she did not read it, for the poet's pleasure lies in his being able to have the last word. Therefore, the personality of the woman plays a part in our enjoyment of the poem; if we know her as high-handed, haughty, promiscuous, and perhaps vindictive, then we can feel pleasure with the poet as he rehearses her "skittish deedes" in his verse, even though it is not the courteous thing to do.

The eternizing theme—the poet immortalizing his mistress in verse—is not strong in Gascoigne; but it is one of the favorite devices of poets throughout the century and certainly one of their most successful. This theme, which is mainly Ovidian, also does not appear often in Petrarch.[11] There are only a few direct statements of it, it is suggested in many of his poems, but nowhere is it substantially developed. In "Sonnet in Death," CCLVI and CCLXXXIII, the theme appears as follows:

> . . . and if I am late to follow,
> Perhaps it will be seen that her dear name
> I shall make sacred with this weary pen.[12]

> And if my rhymes are good for any aim,
> They shall inscribe among the holy merits
> The eternal remembrance of your name.[13]

and in "Sonnet in Life," LXXXIII:

> The rooted virtue that blossomed in you
> When Love began to battle at your door,
> Now bears the fruit where once the flower grew,
> And so my hope can come and touch the shore.

> Therefore my heart begs me to write and tell
> On paper what brings glory to your name;
> For in no other stuff we carve so well
> To make a marble of a living frame.

Think you that Caesar or Marcellus then,
And Paul and Africanus were such men
Thanks to a hammer's or an anvil's strength?

My Pandolfo, those works have no great length,
They are too frail, our own studies are what
Makes men immortal and famous their lot.[14]

This theme in Petrarch is at once tender and didactic; when
he uses it, he warmly compliments his mistress, and he also
expresses one of the values of writing verse. The eternizing
theme is handled differently by Gascoigne, as in the following
sonnet:

These rustie walles whome cankred yeares deface,
The comely corps of seemely *Zouche* enclose,
Whose auncient stocke, derivde from worthy race,
Procures hir prayse, where so the carkas goes:
Hir angels face declares hir modest mynde,
Hir lovely lookes the gazing eyes allure,
Hir deedes deserve some endless prayse to fynde,
To blaze suche brute as ever might endure.
Wherfore my penne in trembling feare shall staye,
To write the thing that doth surmounte my skill,
And I will wishe of God both night and day,
Some worthier place to guyde hir wirthie will.
Where princes peeres hir due desertes may see,
And I content hir servant there to bee.
                                          (Prouty, 146)

The sense of age and death is effected well through the images
of the poem, and, as an exercise in diction, the poem is quite
successful. Gascoigne tries to create a feeling of death, thereby
making the need for some kind of deathless glory more emphatic.
He does not explain, as Petrarch does, the value of preserving
a name in verse; but, through such words as "rustic walles,"
"cankred yeares," "corps," and "carkas," he approaches the emotion underlying the eternizing theme more closely than does
Petrarch, who uses it more as a compliment to his lady than as
a balm for the woes of life's end. It is unfortunate that Gascoigne
does not return to this theme, for he grasps its underlying
characteristics quite well; but he just touches this one Petrarchan
theme and then lets it go by.

Another dissimilarity between Gascoigne and Petrarch is the
attitude each takes toward the poem he is writing. Petrarch very

often speaks directly to his verse, as to a separate person, referring to it familiarly, at times affectionately, as in Song X—"Canzone, I feel my pen already tired/ Of this long and sweet reasoning with her,/ But my thoughts are not tired my talk to share"—[15] and as in Song XXI:

> Flee the clearness, the green,
> Do not go near where there is song and laughter,
> Canzone, follow after
> Weeping; you are not fit for merry folk,
> A widow, without comfort, in black cloak.[16]

And in "Sonnet in Death," CCLXXXVII:

> Go my sorrowful rhymes, to the hard stone
> Where my dear treasure in the earth absconds;
> And then call her, who from heaven responds,
> Although the mortal in the dark is gone.
>
> Tell her that I am tired of life's false vows....[17]

The song takes on a separate personality; to him, it is a companion through whose means he can relieve himself of his passions and sorrows. To Gascoigne, the poem is only an instrument—to be used as a compliment, a petition, and so forth. It is always a possession of the poet, never apart from him; and Gascoigne refers to it as "these verses of mine," or "my pleading rhymes." The effect of Petrarch's technique is that of immediate familiarity with the poet's state of mind as though it had been overheard in dialogue; it establishes an almost discursive tone. Gascoigne's technique puts the reader into the poem and allows more narration and drama, less exposition.

Gascoigne used some of what Petrarch brought to the sixteenth century, but his success as a poet is not dependent on the use of the conventions. He used them less than did the poets of *Tottel's Miscellany*; and, when he did, he was usually aware of their faded efficacy and took it into account in his poems, or else he utilized them as part of a greater whole. He very seldom made his poems merely vehicles for the expression of the Petrarchan conceits. Unlike most of the poets after Wyatt, he did not just copy Petrarch; he learned from him. As a result, a critical position which simply dismisses Gascoigne's poetry as being a poor contribution to the Petrarchan vogue misses much of the beauty and the very real poetical triumphs which the following chapter points out.

CHAPTER 3

The Love Lyrics

A discussion of Gascoigne's lyric poems falls naturally into two sections, those concerning love and those concerning his insights into himself and his society. The love lyrics grew out of his life at court, and they include the forms we expect from the courtly love tradition, such as the praise of a lady, the disclosure of love, and the lament of an absent lover. However, a number of his love lyrics deal with the psychology of love. For example, the absent-lover's lament was usually an exercise in rhetoric, but Gascoigne turns it into an examination of the feelings inherent in the situation. Again, Gascoigne was quite concerned with aging, and in his poetry he reflects the basic, real emotions of an aging lover instead of the pleasant moralizing which we usually find written on this theme. Gascoigne wrote much courtly love poetry, but his most interesting poems focus on the individual rather than on the convention.

In his other lyrics, Gascoigne attempted to understand himself or to orient what he saw around him to his own sense of values. The resulting conflict produced several disturbing lyrics which border on satire, as well as two longer poems—"The Complaint of the green knight" and "Gascoigne's wodmanship"—which look into the poet's own mind and personality for answers to his perplexing problems. In this section of his poems, Gascoigne seeks truth; and the poetry is much less concerned with decoration or sweetness of expression than with accuracy of statement. Therefore, in the second group of Gascoigne's lyrics, those not concerned primarily with love, whatever there is of poetic beauty in the poems comes largely from the degree of accuracy with which he touches the emotions or truths he examines. The expression is secondary, but in his better poems it is restrained and economical, and there are lines which achieve great poetic power as a result of his restraint.

Gascoigne's lyrics create or explore a wide variety of emotions. They include humor, pathos, bitterness, helpless irony, sensuality, light praise, and others. Also, with a few exceptions, his lyrics speak in a definite voice; they are seldom bland or frivolous. The poet's voice is heard in irony, cynicism, lusty pleasure, pessimism, or scorn. At times, his tone interferes with the mood his poem— through imagery or description—has established. But the tone is Gascoigne's peculiar signature to his poems, and it is basically pessimistic. When it interrupts the mood, as in "Spreta tamen viiunt," it impairs the poem's effect; but, when it supports the mood, as in "Lullabye of a lover," the result is highly successful. The wide variety of mood and the consistent and dominant tone, or poetic voice, are characteristics which make Gascoigne distinct from many of the poets of his age.

In this chapter, for the sake of convenience and also to avoid unnecessary conflict, I use the term "lyric" in its loosest sense. I include in it all his poems concerning any aspect of love. But, even more broadly, I exclude from it only *The Steele Glas*, the narrative poems such as "Gascoigne's voyage into Holland," and "Dan Bartholomew of Bath" (although I do refer to his "Last will and Testament"), and the didactic poems such as "Dulce Bellum Inexpertis" (perhaps more appropriately narrative), and "Counsell to Douglas Dive." The body of poems could be broken into smaller and more cogent segments, but my purpose is to analyze them rather than to divide and classify them. Therefore, I use the term "lyric" rather broadly and as a means to classify largely instead of minutely.

I *The Rhetoric of Love*

Although the relationship between the love poetry of Petrarch and that of Gascoigne was discussed in Chapter 2, a few points should be reiterated here. The first is that, when Gascoigne attempted to copy Petrarch's method, his poetry is generally unsuccessful. For example, his poem, "The shield of Love" on the theme of absence, is a general adaptation of a Petrarchan sonnet. In it he manages to work out a rather pleasing courtly figure: "That trustie targe hath long borne off the blowes,/ And broke the thrusts which absence at me throwes." Yet, he was compelled to use well-worn Petrarchan phrases, and the development of the theme is subjugated to them:

> In dolefull dayes I lead an absent life,
> And wound my will with many a weary thought:

> I plead for peace, yet sterve in stormes of strife,
> I find debate, where quiet rest was sought. . . .
>
> So that I live, and dye in one degree,
> Healed by hope, and hurt againe with dread:
> Fast bound by fayth when fansie would be free,
> Untyed by trust, though thoughts enthrall my head:
> Reviv'd by joyes, when hope doth most abound,
> And yet with grief, in depth of dollors drownd.
> (Prouty, 142-43)

The expression is by no means unpleasing, but the content is trite and the conceit worked out in the beginning of the poem is almost completely neglected.

Also, Gascoigne often satirized the Petrarchan conventions in his love poetry. The poem, "The passion of a Lover," suggests such an attitude; but in that poem his treatment of the conventions is mild. However, he handles the Petrarchan tradition most rudely in his "Anatomye of a lover." In this poem, love reduces the lover limb by limb to the state of a wretched corpse. The exaggeration of the conventional effects of love turns the usually applied compliments to the lady into ugly ridicule, and it emphasizes the inherent insipidity of the whole tradition of Petrarchan copying during this part of the century:

> To make a lover knowne, by plaine Anatomie,
> You lovers all that list beware, lo here behold you me. . . .
> These locks that hang unkempt, these hollowe dazled eyes,
> These chattring teeth, this trembling tongue, wel tewed
>   with careful cries.
> These wan & wrinkled cheeks, wel washt with waves of wo,
> May stand for patterne of a ghost, where so this carkasse
>   go. . . .
> My thighes, my knees, my legs, and last of all my feete,
> To serve a lovers turne, are so unable and unmeete, . . .
> Yet for a just rewarde of love so dearely bought,
> I pray you say, lo this was he, whom love had worne to
>   naught.   (Prouty, 143-44)

In most of the love poetry, however, Gascoigne exhibits very little of the Petrarchan influence. His love poems offer a wide variety of types ranging from the most earthy, at times bawdy poems, to delicate, almost philosophical statements on love. In his "Certayne notes of Instruction," Gascoigne mentions several points concerning the writing of love poetry. His first note—"The

first and most necessarie poynt that ever I found meete to be
considered in making of a delectable poeme is this, to grounde
it upon some fine invention."—establishes the importance which
he placed upon the "invention" or conceit of a poem; we see
him developing it in the bed-grave analogy in "Gascoignes good
nyghte," in the figure of a court of law in "Gascoignes araignement," and in the metaphor of a crow in "Counsell to Douglas
Dive." But the poetry of love and compliment offers more difficulty in expressing the intended mood and meaning, so he
elaborates on the problem:

If I should undertake to wryte in prayse of a gentlewoman, I would
neither praise hir christal eye, nor hir cherrie lippe, &c. For these
things are *trita* & *obvia*. But I would either find some supernaturall
cause wherby my penne might walke in the superlative degree, or
els I would undertake to aunswere for any imperfection that shee
hath, and thereupon rayse the prayse of hir commendacion. Likewise
if I should disclose my pretence in love, I would eyther make a
straunge discourse of some intollerable passion, or finde occasion to
pleade by the example of some historie, or discover my disquiet in
shadowes *per Allegoriam,* or use the covertest meane that I could to
avoyde the uncomely customes of comon writers. (Cunliffe, I, 465-66)

The poem "An absent lover thus complayneth" demonstrates his
"occasion to pleade by the example of some historie," as does
"The lover disdaynefully rejected," in which he uses the example
of Angelica and the ever-present Cressida to expose the shortcomings of his once-possessed mistress:

> If *Cressides* name were not so knowen,
> And written wyde on every wall;
> If brute of pryde were not so blowen
> Upon *Angelica* withall:
> For hault disdain thou mightst be she,
> Or *Cressyde* for inconstancie.
>   (Prouty, 131)

Another use of historical example, but with the intent instead
to heighten the fame of the mistress, is the poem "Another
shorter discourse":

> If ever man yit found the Bath of perfect blisse,
> Then swim I now amid the Sea where nought but pleasure is.
> I love and am beloved (without vaunt be it told)
> Of one more fayre than shee of *Grece* for whom proud
>   Troy was sold:

> As bountifull and good as *Cleopatra* Queene:
> As constant as *Penelope* unto hir make was seene.
> What would you more? my pen unable is to write
> The least desart that seemes to shine within this worthy
>   wight.
> So that for now I cease, with hands held up on hye,
> And crave of God that when I chaunge, I may be forst to dye.
>
> (Prouty, 131)

The two instructions which he gives for praising a gentle-woman in poetry are exemplified by the poems "This Praise of a Countess" and by "Gascoigne's prayse of *Bridges*, now Ladie *Sandes*." The first poem devises a "supernaturall cause whereby my penne might walke in the superlative degree." The poet calls upon the gods to help him praise his lady, but they refuse for several reasons, the first of which is jealousy: "For Pallas. . . ./ if once my Ladies gifts were knowen,/ *Pallas* should loose the prayses of hir own." The second reason is love:

> And bloudy *Mars* by chaunge of his delight
> Hath made *Joves* daughter now myne enemie. . . .
> She may go home to *Vulcane* now agayne:
> For Mars is sworne to be my Ladies swayne.

The third reason is loss of power: "Of hir bright beams *Dan Phoebus* stands in dread, . . ./ Dame *Cynthia* holds in her horned head,/ For feare to loose by like comparison" (Prouty, 129-30). The poet here uses the gods themselves to bring about the courtly compliment.

The second poem is an excellent example of the poet's using an imperfection in his lady to heighten his commendation of her. First, Gascoigne refers directly to the disfigurement, and then suggests a supernatural cause for it:

> Although some lavishe lippes, which like some other best,
> Will say the blemishe on hir browe disgraceth all the rest:
> Thereto I thus replie, God wotte they little knowe
> The hidden cause of that mishap, nor how the harm did grow.
>
> (Prouty, 146)

The poet then explains that Bridges' face was so fair that she kindled love in Cupid's breast. But his love quickly turned to hate when Cupid realized how busy she would make him and in anger, "with mightie mace, gan rap her on the pate." Thus, the mark is the symbol of her perfection; and, far from being ugly, she was saved by Nature:

> And quick with skin she covered it, yt whiter is than snow.
> Wherwith *Dan Cupide* fled, for feare of further flame,
> When angell like he saw hir shine, whome he had smit
>   with shame. . . .
> The skar still there remains, no force, there let it be,
> There is no cloud that can eclipse so bright a sunne as she.

The device is cleverly worked out; and, by following his own advice, he creates a worthy compliment that, by another method, could have been quite awkward.

In contrast to Gascoigne's comments in his "Certayne notes," some modern critics maintain that Elizabethan love poetry emphasizes the physical symptoms of love above all other aspects. One says:

To the Elizabethans . . . the expression "lovesick" meant literally what it said. . . . Literary characters affected by it are physically disordered and mentally unbalanced. Some of them go mad. Some of them die. In large part the Elizabethans owed their ideas concerning the love malady to psychological and medical theory. . . . Sometimes love is a hot and excited condition of body and mind which spurs to action; sometimes it is a cold, weak, and passive debility. In the first stage, desire is the dominant passion; in the second, grief is the dominant passion.[1]

This excerpt creditably describes some of the mid-century poetry, but it does not indicate that many of these characteristics stem in part from an overemphasis of the Petrarchan convention of the suffering lover. Such criticism tends to overlook the period's non-Petrarchan love poetry; as a result, it misses the point and, of course, the value of much of the poetry.

The principles of "Certayne notes of Instruction" that we have mentioned are rhetorical ones familiar to every schoolboy of the period. Such techniques are used by the orator, or expository writer, to support and amplify a contention. Gascoigne puts the techniques into a metrical form. His purpose is at least as much to persuade as to delight; he is at least as much concerned with the result as with the means. Thus, when Gascoigne recites his woes, he uses them as a base for presenting a lesson or a truth, the ultimate aim of the poem. In the poem beginning "When I recorde within my musing mind/ The noble

names of wights bewitched in love," his intent is to find a sense
of security, even peace, in the fact that great men in history
suffered in the same way. To prove his contention, he cites David
and Bathsheba, Solomon and the Pharaoh's daughter, Holoferne
and Judith, and Sampson and Delilah—all from biblical times;
and he mentions Nasoes, Corinna, and Cressida from Classical
times to emphasize the all-inclusiveness of love's weakening
power. His final verse recites the lesson to be drawn from his
examples:

> So that to end my tale as I began,
> I see the good, the wise, the stoute, the bolde:
> The strongest champion and the learnedst man,
> Have bene and be, by lust of love controlde.
> Which when I thinke, I hold me well content
> To live in love, and never to repent.
>
> (Prouty, 142)

In his love poetry Gascoigne also often seeks out an intellectual
relationship between the lover and the conditions of love. He
states his contention, searches for supporting evidence, and
draws conclusions that are psychologically sound, as in the
poem, "The lamentation of a lover":

Now have I found the waye, to weepe & wayle my fill,
Now can I end my dolefull dayes, & so content my will.
The way to weepe inough, for such as list to wayle,
Is this: to go abord ye ship, where pleasure beareth sayle.
And there to mark the jestes of every joyfull wight,
And with what wynde and wave they fleete, to nourish their delight.
For as the striken Deare, that seeth his fellowes feede
Amid the lustie heard (unhurt) & feeles himself to bleede.
Or as the seely byrd, that with the Bolte is brusd,
And lieth a loofe among the leaves, of al hir peeres refusd,
And heares them sing full shrill, yet cannot she rejoyce,
Nor frame one warbling note to pass out of hir mournfull voyce.
Even so I find by proofe, that pleasure dubleth payne
Unto a wretched wounded hart, which doth in woe remaine.
I passe where pleasure is, I heare some sing for joye,
I see som laugh, some other daunce, in spight of darke anoy.
But out alas my mind amends not by their myrth,
I deeme al pleasures to be paine, that dwel above ye earth.
Such heavy humors feede, ye bloud that lends me breath,
As mery medcins cannot serve, to kepe my corps from death.

(Prouty, 123-24)

This poem shows quite clearly the pattern Gascoigne uses to develop the statements he makes in many of his love poems. The contention, or truth, of the above poem is stated in the third and fourth lines. (He usually uses a metaphor or an analogy for the poetic effect.) Then he discovers examples from other aspects of life to heighten and establish the soundness of the second key statement of the truth, "I finde by proofe that pleasure doubleth payne/ Unto a wretched wounded hart." The transition from the examples to the poet is simply made with "I pass where pleasure is," and from that point on the reader is brought to know one precise reality in the world of a lover.

II *Love and Mutability*

Gascoigne follows the same rhetorical pattern in his poem upon the theme, *Spreta tamen viuunt;* but he plunges more deeply into a type of stoical philosophy here. Again, he begins the poem with a statement of an observed truth: "Despysed things may live, although they pine in payne,/ And things ofte trodden under foote may once yet rise againe"; and he develops it with a number of examples, such as "The rootes of rotten Reedes in swelling seas are seen,/ And when eche tide hath tost his worst, they grow again ful greene." But this theme is only preparatory to the major one; for the poet has been cast aside by his love, and, in order to learn, as did "trustie Troylus," to accept his fate, he asks for help from philosophy. Thus, the poet is launched on his deeper theme, one which fully supports the theme at the poem's start:

I see no sight on earth but it to Chaunge enclines:
As little clowds oft overcast, the brightest sunne that shines.
No Flower is so fresh, but frost can it deface:
No man so sure in any seate but he maye leese his place.
So that I stand content (though much against my mind)
To take in worth this lothsome lot, which luck to me assynd,
And trust to see the time, when they that nowe are up:
May feele the whirle of fortunes wheele, and tast of sor-
      rowes cup.
God knoweth I wish it not, it had ben bet for mee:
Still to have kept my quiet chayre in hap of high degree.
But since without recure, Dame Chaunge in love must raigne:
I now wish chaunge that sought no chaunge, but constant
      did remain.
And if such chaunge do chance, I vowe to clap my hands,

> And laugh at them which laught at me: lo thus my fansy
>   stands.   (Prouty, 126-27)

The question of thwarted love is secondary to the all-inclusiveness of the philosophical truth of mutability. The poet instinctively recognizes the depth of his theme, and in only three lines he applies it to the whole range of life: the "brightest sunne," the sixteenth-century symbol of kingship, is checked or overthrown by a little cloud; the "Flower" is youth or life which is snuffed out by "frost" or death;[2] and one "sure in any seate" has worldly power or fame which can suffer sudden change. In the face of this truth, the poet knows he can do no more than wait and watch and at the same time review his misfortunes. The line "I now wish chaunge that sought no chaunge, but constant did remaine" is a pleasant play on words in which the poet would like his unhappy mood to pass in accordance with the principle of change so that he could escape. Thus, Gascoigne has proved that hope is an ever-present condition, at least in lovers, and that its philosophical basis is the principle of mutability.

The somewhat cynical tone near the end of the poem which appears in his desire to see the high brought low and in his wish to have the last laugh makes this poem more than just one about vagaries of love. In fact, the tone conflicts with the message of hope that the poet wants to convey; and it does so because the poet is so bitter about the way life has handled him that he cannot keep the expression of it out of his poems. We see it in "Lullaby of a lover," in "The divorce of a lover," in "Gascoignes wodmanship," and in many others; it appears as cynicism, bitterness, and pessimism.

His pessimism is often reflected in his expression of the lover-loved one relationship. The poem "The Partridge in the pretie Merlines foot" is a love poem which uses an analogy to make clear the terms of the lover's involvement. In the first half of the poem, the partridge, who is the lover, has been caught in the foot of the Merlin plant and finds herself prey to the hawk above and to the dogs below. Her wings, therefore, cannot save her from the dogs, and her protective coloring does not hide her from the hawk; her position is hopeless because of the Merlin: "But nature made the Merlyne mee to kyll,/ And me to yeeld unto the Merlines will." The poet then compares his state in each respect to the preceding description:

> Desire thy dogge, did spring me up in hast:
> Thou wert the Hauke, whose tallents caught me fast. . . .
>
> Thou are that Hauke, whom nature made to hent me,
> And I the Byrd, that must therewith content me.
>
> And since Dame Nature hath ordayned so,
> Her happie heast I gladly shall embrace:
> I yeeld my will, although it were to wo,
> I stand content to take my griefe for grace: . . .
>
> (Prouty, 121)

The point of interest here is the concept underlying the analogy: the lover is the helpless prey; the loved one, a cruel bird of prey. The Merlin, usually a symbol of lust, suggests the whole condition of love as a trap. Desire is a low animal, a dog, which forces the lover into the trap; physical charms are cruel and deadly. Yet, the situation is natural and, therefore, to be accepted. There is a complete absence of chivalric or romantic ideals of love in the poem; nature, the very terms of existence, is cruel and devouring. Even the greatest pleasure, physical love, brings pain; it is described in terms of captive and tormentor; and it can be accepted only fatalistically, without joy and, ultimately, without hope.

The group of poems which lament the absence of a lover, although quite conventional, maintain the pessimistic tone of Gascoigne's poetry. Such complaints have been a familiar poetic theme, extending at least as far back as the early French Troubadors; and Gascoigne has some success with it. The lamenting lover may be either male or female, but we would expect the woman's lament to be more poignant as she can do nothing but wait, whereas the man has available to him at least the distractions of worldly business. As a result, when the poet assumes the woman's point of view, his poem is usually more successful than with the man's. With Gascoigne, this observation certainly holds. In one lament in which he takes the man's position, he produces one of his tritest, most poorly written poems. The poem shows a lover bidding his lady to be patient; the first verse contains the inanity which is diffused throughout the poem:

> Content thy selfe with patience perforce,
> And quench no love with droppes of darke mistrust:
> Let absence have no power to divorce,

> Thy faithfull freend which meaneth to be just.
> Beare but a while thy constance to declare,
> For when I come one ynche shall breake no square.
> (Prouty, 136-37)

The applicability of the last line leaves a little doubt. Further on, apparently running out of material, Gascoigne again resorts to nonsense:

> Be thou a true *Penelope* to me,
> And thou shalt soone thine owne *Ulisses* see.

> What sayd I? soone? yea, soone I saye againe;
> I wyll come soone, and sooner if I may:

Finally, he resorts to the Petrarchan tradition: " I fryse in hope, I thaw in hot desire,/ Farre from the flame, and yet I burne like fire." Yet even in such a worthless poem as this one, Gascoigne leaves his stamp upon the reader in his directness and in his attempt to express a truth, as given in the last verse:

> Wherfore deare friend, thinke on the pleasures past,
> And let my teares, for both our paynes suffise:
> The lingring joyes, when as they come at last,
> Are bet then those, which passe in posting wise.
> And I my selfe, to prove this tale is true,
> In hast, post hast, thy comfort will renew.

Gascoigne has significantly better success, as we have noted, when he assumes the woman's point of view. In his poem, "The vertue of *Ver*," although some of the beauty is stifled by his constant use of "Ver" in place of "Spring," his poetic technique is skillfully displayed. Gascoigne forms a framework around the central figure, a woman bewailing her lack of love, by having the poet approach her in a boat and overhear the lament; at the end, he hurries home to write the poem. The device is successful because it heightens the essential contrasts and levels of the poem—winter and spring, fertility and barrenness, gaiety and grief. The poet, as he sees that spring has come, "... crost the *Thames* to take the cherefull ayre/ In open feeldes...." As he approaches the opposite shore, he hears weeping and investigates:

> Alas (quod she) behold eche pleasaunt greene,
> Will now renew, his sommers livery;

The fragrant flowers, which have not long bene seene,
Will florish now, (ere long) in bravery:
The tender buddes, whom colde hath long kept in,
Will spring and sproute, as they do now begin.

But I (alas) within whose mourning mind
The graffes of grief, are onely given to growe,
Cannot enjoy the spring which others finde,
But still my will must wyther all in woe:
The cold of care so nippes my joyes at roote,
No sunne doth shine that well can do them boote.

The lustie *Ver*, which whillome might exchange
My griefe to joy, and then my joyes encrease,
Springs now elsewhere, and showes to me but strange,
My winters woe, therefore can never cease:
In other coasts his sunne full clere doth shine,
And comfort lends to ev'ry mould but mine.
                                        (Prouty, 122-23)

Gascoigne shows a sensitivity to nature here that can be compared to Surrey's sonnet on spring that we quoted in the previous
chapter. And he achieves a poignant irony in the verse beginning
"But I, alas!" The poem captures the idea of fertility and birth
which sets off the barrenness and hints of frigidity in the woman.
The subject of the poem is unusual, for the woman has not
merely lost a lover; she is incapable of love. She "Cannot enjoy
the spring which others finde." The fact that her desire ("will")
must wither and the words "The lustie *Ver* . . . showes to me but
strange" suggest frigidity in the woman. The point is given a
humorous turn as the lady blushes deeply upon discovering her
spy: "By sight whereof, Lord, how she chaunged hew!/ So
that for shame I turned backe apace." But the blush and the
poet's shame at what he heard, rather than his sympathy or
pity, again reinforce the suggestion of frigidity. It is strange that
Gascoigne would write about this subject, but the poem undeni-
ably presents effective contrasts on several levels of perception,
and the most effective is the image of the frigid woman unable
to receive warmth or life from the burgeonings around her.

In the poem "An absent Dame thus complayneth" nothing
complicates the personality of the woman; she is simply waiting
at home while her lover is away. Gascoigne makes the situation
clear, for the woman says explicitly:

> The droppes of dark disdayne, did never drench my hart,
> For well I know I am belov'd, if that might ease my smart.
> Ne yet the privy coales, of glowing jellosie
> Could ever kindle needlesse feare, within my fantasie.
> The rigor of repulse, doth not renew my playnt,
> Nor choyce of change doth move my mone, nor force me
>   thus to faynt,
> Onely that pang of payne, which passeth all the rest,
> And cankerlike doth fret the hart, within the giltlesse brest.
>   (Prouty, 125)

The mood or emotion of the woman is developed through a series of similes showing various aspects of her situation, as in the two below:

> Much like the seely Byrd, which close in Cage is pent,
> So sing I now, not notes of joye, but layes of deepe lament.
> And as the hooded Hauke, which heares the Partrich spring,
> Who though she feele hir self fast tyed, yet beats hir bating wing:
> So strive I now to showe, my feeble forward will, . . .

The images can be analyzed to show explicitly the feelings which mingle within the woman. The frivolous, lighthearted bird contrasts dramatically with the hooded hawk and heightens the loss which each figure represents—the caged bird, joy; the hawk, sexual desire ("my feeble forward will"). Further on, she sings "Swallow-like,"—in a single plaintive note not sweet or joyful. The use of bird images to describe a woman left alone allows the reader to penetrate deeply into her emotions—her sadness, and her strong but blunted desire—and to determine to some extent their tone. However, the poem introduces other images—a greyhound restrained from chasing his game, love as seeds being sown and reaped—which destroy the poem's unity and nearly obliterate the good effects of the bird similes.

The most successful of this group of poems is "A Lady, being both wronged by false suspect . . ." in which Gascoigne suggests the accompaniment of a lute, with its occasional loud strums and twangs, as a sound background to the woman's frustrated emotions. He establishes the scene in the first verse and carries it throughout the entire poem:

> Give me my Lute in bed now as I lye,
> And lock the doores of mine unluckie bower:
> So shall my voyce in mournefull verse descrie,
> The secrete smart which causeth me to lower.

Resound, you walles an Eccho to my mone,
And thou, cold bed wherein I lie alone:
Beare witness yet what rest thy Lady takes,
When other sleepe which may enjoy their makes.

(The following five stanzas describe in order the first bloom
of love and happiness, the slander and discord begun by persons
envious of her state, the loss of her husband's confidence, and
"the greatest grief of all"—her being forcibly kept from seeing
her husband.)

Now have you heard the summe of all my grief,
Whereof to tell my hart (oh) rends in twayne:
Good Ladies yet lend you me some relief,
And beare a parte to ease me of my payne.
My sortes are such, that waying well my trueth,
They might provoke the craggy rocks to rueth,
And move these walles with teares for to lament,
The lothsome life wherin my youth is spent.

But thou, my Lute, be stil; now take thy rest,
Repose thy bones upon this bed of downe:
Thou hast dischargd some burden from my breast,
Wherefore take thou my place, here lie thee downe.
And let me walke to tyre my restlesse minde,
Untill I may entreate some curteous wynde:
To blow these wordes unto my noble make,
That he may see I sorowe for his sake.

(Prouty, 133-35)

Several places in the poem demand a sudden, loud strumming
on the lute, as in the fifth line of the first stanza. The effect is
that of a lute accompanying a sort of chant, producing a descant;
and we can literally find levels of volume which stand for peaks
of emotion in the singer. At the beginning, the woman is over-
wrought and loud; she is compelled to relieve herself through
the descant. In the following stanzas, as she moves from the
emotionally low-pitched history of her marriage through the
appearance of slander and false suspect, she continually increases
in volume, until she hits the peak of her misfortune—her lover's
absence. At this point, she is loud and nearly incoherent; but
she regains control, and the following stanza descends considerably in volume by means of such words as "weary" and "tyre"
until, in that stanza, she gives up the song to her ladies in waiting, but not before she emphasizes one last surge of emotion

with her lute "(oh)." The reference to the good ladies, of course, has a double meaning; not only are they asked to join her song literally, but they are also asked to spread the truth about their mistress. The images in the last stanzas reinforce the emotion very well, particularly when the lute and the woman change places, the lute becoming tired "bones" upon the bed and the woman becoming the restless instrument of a sorrowful melody.

Gascoigne, who does several things quite well in this poem, produces the effect of a musical instrument and uses it to underline the emotional peaks of the poem. He uses alliteration well, in places with great effect. His syntax is not crude nor artificial; in the last stanza, it is highly effective. And his images are vivid and successful. In all the poems of this group, he captures the mood and personality of the women quite accurately and effectively.

A number of Gascoigne's poems concern themselves with the problems of the lover as he grows old and as his capacity for physical love dries up. The stark reality of the loss of youth fills him with mingled feelings of awe and despair; and this pessimism is brought out strongly in the poem "A Lover often warned," in which the poet, as an older man, gains as a reward for his search for love only a "sodain clappe." In the poem, Gascoigne investigates the attitudes felt by a middle-aged man pursuing physical love. The man, who in his youth "had the fieldes of freedome woon,/ And liv'd at large, and playde with pleasurs ball," now desires again to live with the fast, loose crowd of his youth. He says:

> My cares were cold, and craved comforts coale,
> To warme my will with flakes of freendly flame.
> I sought and found, I crav'd and did obtene,
> I woon my wish, and yet I got no gaine.
> (Prouty, 140-41)

His "will," of course, is his lust, or sexual desire, which has diminished as he has grown older. Yet, in his attempts to revive the joys of his youth, he finds that he no longer is able to satisfy himself—"Dame pleasures plasters prov'd a corosive"—and, worse still, he is unable to attract the young women but must rely on those as jaded as he is old:

> The cause is this, my lot did light too late,
> The Byrdes were flowen, before I found the nest: . . .

And I fond foole with emptie hand must call,
The gorged Hauke, which likes no lure at all.

Thus still I toyle, to till the barreyne land,
And grope for grapes among the bramble briers:
I strive to sayle and yet I sticke on sand,
I deeme to live, yet drowne in deep desires.
These lots of love are fitte for wanton will,
Which findes too much, yet must be seeking still.

The metaphors in the concluding stanza transmit the sense of frustration and pathos very effectively. The state of the lover is more than ridiculous; it is hopeless, but he is doomed to continue the game.

In this poem, Gascoigne achieves certain poetic effects that deserve our attention. The "flakes of friendly flame" image is strongly suggestive of metaphysical poetry. The combination of "flame" with "flakes" produces a tension which is resolved only when we realize it is the "coale" which flakes to produce the warmth; for coals, when jostled, break up and shoot out small flames and heat. In terms of the metaphor, the coal is the warm, suggestive gestures and actions of others which the poet as an old man relies upon to arouse passion within himself. This type of intellectual density, one that critics so much admire in the Metaphysical poets, is frequently found in Gascoigne's poetry.

The other effect is contained in the lines: "And I, fond foole, with emptie hand must call,/ The gorged Hauke, which likes no lure at all." Here the poet heightens our sense of his futility by an order of three: first, the empty hand; beyond that, the already sated bird; and, further still, a bird which does not succumb to lures in the first place—and he succeeds without recourse to an artificial method such as hyperbole. Instead, he describes a level, or type of experience which, through metaphor, perfectly describes another level, or type. In expressing the lover's position in this poem, Gascoigne faces the reality of the world; he does not lose himself in a romantic dream. Of course, this reality is pessimistic, and he does not temper this pessimism with the fact that he has gained maturity and wisdom. It is painful to him; it, like the flaws he finds in his society, is another crack in the structure of the world of his youth.

The villain in these poems is time. It causes change and decay in both society and the individual; it is the great destroyer of all things; and it forces man to face the horrors of the grave.

Yet, it is, at the same time, a democratic force, one which
levels all people and all accomplishments. Viewed in this light,
time becomes a teacher; and one who can understand time holds
a certain wisdom which can be spread to others. In a fine long
poem, *The Grief of Joye*, Gascoigne seeks to teach the super-
ficiality of the pleasures found in youth, in beauty, in strength,
and in activity. Each of these pleasures holds its own trap for an
individual; beauty, for example, breeds lust, vanity, and physical
weakness; but the inevitable loss of each pleasure is caused by
the passage of time. He says of youth:

> For youthe cannot, stande still in one estate,
> But flieth us from, when most thereof is made
> And age steales on, unto our privy gate,
> And in ye darke, doth (silently) invade,
> Youthes fortte unwares: wch never knewe y^t trade./
> So: when we thincke, age furthest from our lyfe,
> Youthes doore breakes up, and yt steppes in by strife.
>   (Cunliffe, II, 520)

Of beauty, the greatest grief is to watch it disappear, to see the
eyes become dull, the ivory necks yellow, erect shoulders stoop,
voices become hoarse, and so forth. The cause of all this change
is time:

> And yet all this (in tyme) will come to passe/
> Whiche tyme flyes fast, as I (of late) did singe/
> Yf wee would then, continew y^t wch was,
> Stay tyme (in tyme) before away shee flyng/
> But yf wee cannot, tyme (past) backward bring,
> Then never hope, that *Bewtie* can remayne,
> Yt came wth tyme, and goeth with tyme agayne./
>   (Cunliffe, II, 536)

Strength, or force, is easily overcome:

> Great laboure doth, deminish greatest force,
> And darke dysease, decrease the strength as fast/
> When bothe thes fayle, the mightiest massy corps,
> Ys daunted downe, wth Ages Axe at last/
> So that when wightest wrastlyng tricks be past,
> Coomes crooked Eldd, and geves a selly trypp,
> Tyll from deathes foote, no stowrdy strong can skypp/
>   (Cunliffe, II, 543)

Throughout the poem, the verses discussing time contain the
most effective poetry; they are more concerned with death

than are the other stanzas, and their imagery is stronger. The
two stanzas given below handle the theme in different moods
but with good effect:

> Much lyke to them, who (sitting in a shipp)
> Are borne forthright, and feele no footing sturr./
> In silent sleepes, the tyme awaie dothe slipp./
> Yt neither bawlethe (like a contrie curre)
> Nor standeth styll, to byde a hasty spurre/
> But slily slydes, and never maketh noyse,
> And much bewrayes: with verie little voyce./
> (Cunliffe, II, 523)

> Tell me but this, what mighty man hathe powre,
> To drive S^r deathe, one furlong from his doore?
> What yowthe so strong, as to prolong his hower?
> Or who can salve, S^r surfetts festring soore?
> Ys yt not trewe, that moyling more and more,
> Awake, on sleepe, att ease, or bating breathe,
> Wee steale (by steppes) unto the gates of deathe?
> (Cunliffe, II, 544)

Even though Gascoigne criticizes at length various aspects of
each subject—the boasting and wastefulness of youth, the traps
of beauty mentioned above, the boorishness, recklessness, and
mindlessness of strength, and the foolishnesses and perils of
various activities—he does offer some constructive comments for
each subject. For youth:

> Whereas in deede, most comfort is compiled,
> In things wch seeme, to be but bytter bale/
> Marke well my woordes and trust unto my tale,
> "All is not golde, wch glistereth faire and bright,
> "Nor all things good, wch fairest seeme in sight.
> "Trew joye cannot, in trifleng toyes consist/
> "Nor happines, in joyes wch soone decaie/
> (Cunliffe, II, 524)

and for beauty:

> How muche were better (then) to decke the mynde,
> And make that fayre, whose light might alwaies last?
> Eternall fame, to wysdome is assignd/
> And modesty, dothe purchase praise as fast/ ...

> If Dames demaund, howe they the same might deeme?
> I answere thus: the fayre which is content,

> Withe natures gyftes / and neither dothe esteeme,
> Yt selfe to muche: nor is to lightnes bent,
> Nor woulde be loved, but with a true entent:
> And strives in goodnes, likewise to excell,
> I say thatt *Bewtie,* beares awaie the bell./
>   (Cunliffe, II, 524)

The underlying element in his advice is that man should take pleasure in those personal qualities which aging will not diminish: the qualities of character and mind. There is certainly a strong element of Classical philosophy, particularly Boetheus, in the poem; but Gascoigne also learned from his own experience of growing older, and the lesson thus taught follows quite consistently from the experiences he describes in his lyrics. He shows that he has grasped the essential features of this life— unrelenting change and decay. His lesson is that we must accept these facts, learn from them, and guide our desires accordingly.

Yet Gascoigne himself does not submit to these laws without some regret. In a mood of pessimistic acceptance, he writes the exquisite lyric, "Lullabye of a lover." In it, he lists all that he must give up as he grows old: his youth, his roving and vain eye, his lust, and his potency. The poet writes in the form of a lullaby:

> Sing lullaby, as women do,
> Wherewith they bring their babes to rest, . . .
> Full many wanton babes have I
> Which must be stilld with lullabie.
>   (Prouty, 150-51)

The eight-line iambic tetrameter stanza, with the first four lines cross-rhyming and with the last four rhyming as couplets, has a hushed, muted sound. The repetition of the word "lullaby," appearing several times in each stanza, brings to the poem the effect of crooning, so that on the surface the poem is passive and tender. Yet, in each stanza there is one detail that intrudes into the peaceful tone; for example, he writes of his youth, "For crooked age and hoary heares,/ Have wonne the haven within my head"; on his roving eye, "For every glasse may now suffise,/ To shew the furrowes in my face"; on his lust, "Since all too late I fynde by skill,/ How deare I have thy fansies bought"; and on his potency, "Synce Age is colde, and nothing coye,/ Keepe close thy coyne, for so is beste." The intrusions are the results of growing old, and they describe the reason why each pleasure is now passing. But, to soften the harshness, each detail is followed with the lullaby refrain, as in the stanza on his youth:

> With Lullabye then youth be still,
> With Lullabye content thy will,
> Since courage quayles, and commes behynde,
> Goe sleepe, and so beguyle thy mynde.

Much of the effectiveness of this poem lies in the irony of "Lullabye" and "sleepe." A lullaby is for children and is meant to pacify and to bring to rest. But what the poet means to do is literally to dismiss from his awareness any recognition of youthful pleasures. However, the muted bitterness of the poem arises because he cannot beguile his mind, cannot help regretting bitterly the passing of his earlier joys; and thus what seems to be a pleasant call to sleep is a galling, heavy awareness of reality. The poet gives himself advice which he cannot accept. In the last stanza he, in effect, bids farewell to his pleasures and girds himself for the years of bitterness ahead:

> Thus Lullabie my youth, myne eyes,
> My will, my ware, and all that was,
> I can no mo delayes devise,
> But welcome payne, lette pleasure passe:
> With Lullabye nowe take your leave,
> With Lullabye youre dreames deceyve,
> And when you rise with waking eye,
> Remembre *Gascoignes* Lullabye.

The "welcome payne" and "rise with waking eye" show his complete acceptance of the reality of growing old. There are several ironies in the individual stanzas which show that the poet has learned from bitter experiences, such as finding by skill—that is, from the doctor—that his fancies bring disease now more than pleasure. But the over-all tension results from the conflict between the dreamlike lullaby tone and the harsh, unrelentingly realistic content.

CHAPTER 4

Social and Personal Lyric Poetry

I *The Legal Poems*

A number of poems which Prouty calls "mock-serious" may serve as a transition between the love poems and the social and personal lyrics. Although these poems deal with love, Gascoigne employs a legal terminology which places love against the larger background of law and society. They include "Gascoignes recantation," "Gascoignes libell of Divorce," "Gascoignes araignement," "His libell of request exhibited to Care," and "His last will and Testament." The poems stem from his legal training at Gray's Inn, a training which influenced other poets as well; and the formality of the legal figure in the poems is pronounced, as we see in the "Last will":

> In *Jove* his mightie name, this eight and twentith day,
> Of frosty bearded Januar, the enemie to May:
> Since Adam was create, five thousand yeares I gesse,
> Five hundreth, forty more and five, as stories do expresse.
> I being whole of mind, (immortall Gods have praise)
> Though in my body languishing with pangs of paine alwayes,
> Do thus ordeyne my will which long in woes have wepte,
> Beseeching myne executours to see it duely kepte.
> Firste I bequeath my soule on *Charons* boate to tende, ...
>   (Prouty, 215)

Another example is the "libell of Divorce":

> Divorce me now good death, from love and lingring life,
> That one hath ben my concubine, that other was my wife. ...
> Be judge then gentle death, and take my cause in hand,
> Consider every circumstance, marke how the case doth stande. ...
> Yes gentle judge give eare, ...   (Prouty, 148-49)

The mockery comes through the strangeness of these terms as part of a poem, and there is considerable irony drawn from them. In the "libell of Divorce," Gascoigne asks death to sever

56

him from love and life, whom he calls concubine and wife, respectively. The legal terminology, thus wrenched from its normal usage, provides a curious and effective angle from which to view an otherwise stale subject. The abstraction love takes on the characteristics of a mistress:

> First love, my concubine, whome I have kept so trimme, . . .
> She cast me off long since, and holds me in disdaine, . . .
> The greenesse of my yeares, doth wither now so sore,
> That lusty love leapes quite away, and liketh me no more.

Life, another tenuous concept, becomes vulgarly real as the opposing party. She takes on palpable characteristics and becomes an antagonist, a rather unusual role for life to play:

In lothsome life that crooked croane, although she be my mate?
She cloyes me with the cough, hir comforte is but colde
She bids me give mine age for almes, where first my youth was solde.
No day can passe my head, but she beginnes to brall,
No mery thoughts conceived so fast, but she confounds them all.
When I pretend to please, she overthwarts me still,
When I would faynest part with hir, she overwayes my will.

By the end of the poem, the poet has successfully made real the concepts of love and life as felt by an aging man. The legal phrasing allows him to use personifications in a natural way and to show the strife each causes within a man. We are able to accept the poem on two levels of perception—the literal and the metaphorical—and we are more apt to be sympathetic with than amused at the legal summation near the end:

> Yes gentle judge give eare, and thou shalt see me prove,
> My concubine incontinent, a common whore is love.
> And in my wife I find, such discord and debate,
> As no man living can endure the torments of my state.
> Wherefore thy sentence say, divorce me from them both, . . .

The most successful poem of this group is "Gascoignes araignement," in which a miniature trial is conducted. The success of this poem lies in the poet's ability to establish the allegory, to create the picture of an actual trial, and to keep the poem a light and finely drawn compliment to womanhood. The process of the trial is given in the first four lines:

> At Beauties barre as I did stande,
> When false suspecte accused mee,

> *George* (quod the Judge) holde up thy hande,
> Thou art araygnde of Flatterie:
>
> (Prouty, 144)

Then, after a decision that the proper Justice should preside instead of Beauty herself, the trial by jury begins:

> Then crafte the cryer call'd a queste,
> Of whome was falshode formoste feere,
> A packe of pickethankes were the rest,
> Which came false witnesse for to beare,
> The Jurie such, the Judge unjust,
> Sentence was sayde I shoulde be trust.

Following the trial itself, comes the sentencing:

> *George* (quod the Judge) now thou art cast,
> Thou muste goe hence to heavie hill,
> And there be hangde all but the head,
> God reste thy soule when thou are dead.

And then, in its proper order, comes the appeal for mercy; and all the compliment of the poem is contained here: "You knowe if I have ben untrue,/ It was in too muche praysing you." Beauty relents and decides to bind George to her service for life. Thus, being tried, convicted, and sentenced for the crime of flattery, George must live his life as "Beauties bounden thrall." The contrast between the grave overtones of the trial and the frivolity of the issue produces an effective tension and gives weight to the poet's compliment to beauty. The theme is deftly handled; the effect, pleasing.

II *Social Lyrics*

However, most of Gascoigne's lyric poetry is not light and pleasing. Running thrugh much of his work is a strong awareness of and sensitivity to the existence of a destructive force— on both the personal and the social level. The intellectual side of this awareness forms the basis for his satire, and his emotional reaction to it is a major part of his lyric poetry. This feeling, which almost becomes a poetic theme, is one of disintegration. His awareness of the breakdown of structure or form, either suddenly or gradually, gives him a sense of despair, one at times bordering on terror; and it accounts for the prevailing spirit of pessimism in his poetry.

Specifically, this theme of disintegration in Gascoigne involves his awareness of moral decay, in society and within the individual, and of the physical decay of the body. Deceit and corruption of men; treachery and cowardice among the leaders of armies; infidelity and adultery among the nobles of his country— all present themselves to the poet's eye as the breakdown of moral and traditional forms. As we would expect, the bulk of Gascoigne's writings on the disintegration in the social order is satiric in nature; and his long, somewhat autobiographical poems, such as "Dulce Bellum Inexpertis," contain strong criticisms of both the existing social and moral orders. Yet, certain of his lyric poems reflect the same sense of disappointment with the world of society.

The first group of poems we shall discuss were written about Gascoigne's experiences at court, the period during which he first felt that the world was not as it seemed to be. The seven linked sonnets on the theme of *Sat cito, si sat bene* describe the period; the first sonnet describes those expectations which soon became blunted; and, through these lines, we can hear the heavily ironic voice of the poet in reflection:

> In haste, poste haste, when fyrste my wandring mynde,
> Behelde the glistring Courte with gazing eye,
> Suche deepe delyghtes I seemde therein to fynde,
> As myght beguile a graver guest than I.
> The stately pompe of Princes and their peeres,
> Did seeme to swimme in flouddes of beaten golde,
> The wanton world of yong delightfull yeeres,
> Was not unlyke a heaven for to beholde,
> Wherin did swarme (for every saint) a Dame,
> So faire of hue, so freshe of their attire,
> As might excell dame *Cinthia* for Fame,
> Or conquer *Cupid* with his owne desire.
> These and suche lyke were baytes that blazed still
> Before myne eye to feede my greedy will.
> (Prouty, 155)

The final couplet emphasizes the poet's awareness of his own shortcomings and how court life exploited them. He returns to this theme several times in his autobiographical lyrics. If some brusque humor appears in these sonnets, it is dissipated by the general tone of stultification and outrage. Gascoigne found no room at court for a straightforward and honest man; he was affected by the unconcern of court society for the real values of

life, by its preoccupation with temporary and superficial things.
He found, instead, small deceits, little pleasures, pointless ridicule. In these sonnets, Gascoigne suggests that the appetite of
the figures at court is insatiable, and that no amount of foolish
spending, duelling, or petty intriguing could satisfy it. When
he ran out of money, he was finally brought to his senses:

> But when this hotte accompte was coldely scande,
> I thought high time aboute me for to looke:
> With heavie cheare I cast my head abacke,
> To see the fountayne of my furious race,
> Comparde my losse, my livyng, and my lacke,
> In equall balance with my jolye grace,
> And sawe expences grating on the grounde
> Lyke lumpes of leade to presse my pursse full ofte,
> When lyghte rewarde and recompence were founde,
> Fleeting lyke feathers in the wynde alofte: . . .
>
> (Prouty, 156-57)

The blame is not on the court but on Gascoigne's failure to understand the requirements of such a life.

Several years later, in "The Fruit of Fetters," he again attempts
to understand his failure at court. This time he sees "Fansie"
as the cause of his mistakes:

> The glosse of gorgeous courtes, by thee did please mine eye,
> A stately sight me thought it was, to see the brave go by:
> To see their feathers flaunte, to marke their straunge devise,
> To lie alonge in Ladies lappes, to lispe and make it nice:
> To fawne and flatter both, I liked sometimes well,
> But since I see how vayne it is, *Fansie* (quoth he), *farewell*.
>
> (Cunliffe, I, 380)

In spite of the overtones of sarcasm, Gascoigne accepts all
blame to himself. The court is as it must be; he does not pass
judgment on it, at least not in his lyrics. Instead, he finds a
principle within himself which caused him to fail at everything
he tried over the years: at love ("Thou madste me live in love
which wisedome biddes me hate"), at farming ("When court
had cast me off, I toyled at the plowe"), at hunting ("In hunting of the deere my fansie tooke delight"), at poetry ("A fansie
fedde me once to wryte in verse and rime"), and at war ("*Fansie*
[quoth he] *farewell*, which made me follow drommes"). All that
is left for him is a stoical acceptance of his fate and a hope for
something better:

If reason rule my thoughts, and God vouchsafe me grace,
Then comfort of Philosophie, shall make me chaunge my race:
And fonde I shall it finde, that Fansie settes to showe,
For weakely stands that building still, which lacketh grace bylow:
But since I must accept my fortunes as they fell,
I say, God send me better speede, and *Fansie now farewell.*
(Cunliffe, I, 381)

Eventually, Gascoigne's failures at court forced him into the relatively sincere profession of soldiering; but, as his experience broadened, he found that society's corruption touched him even there. This discovery erupted in a series of lyrical, auto-biographical, and satirical poems; and one quite interesting one is the strange "Epitaph upon Captain Bourchier." In it, the speaker is a stone, a device intended to suggest that man's heart is harder than even rock:

Now muze not reader though we stones can speake,
Or write sometimes the deedes of worthy ones,
I could not hold although my heart should breake,
Bycause here by me buried are his bones,
But I must tell this tale thus for the nones.
When men crie mumme and keepe such silence long,
Then stones must speake, els dead men shall have wrong.
(Prouty, 171-72)

The poet is embittered because society so quickly forgets the men who fought and died in its defense—a neglect so heinous that even the stones must speak out, although a bit self-consciously. In several of the stanzas he names the traditional values possessed by Bourchier—courage, modesty, fidelity—and suggests an ironic contrast between Bourchier and the country-men he defended:

Bourcher is dead, whom eche of you did knowe,
Yet no man writes one worde to paint his praise,
His sprite on high, his carkasse here belowe,
Doth both condemne your doting idle dayes: . . .
He might for birth have boasted noble race,
Yet were his manners meeke and always milde. . . .
In fielde a lion, and in towne a childe.

The barbed contrast in the last line quoted is delivered with authority and indicates that Gascoigne is certain of his position as a judge; he is able clearly to contrast his values with those of a thoughtless society more interested in rewards than in values.

Beneath its elegiac tone, the poem reflects Gascoigne's own reaction to the treatment he had received as a soldier. Although he was disillusioned, humiliated, and angered, his attention is directed at concrete wrongs outside himself. He has not yet experienced that breadth of vision which, as it forced his eye inward, developed in him feelings of failure and despair—feelings he attempted to understand and dispel in his later lyrics. When such a development did occur, it represented more than anything else a summing up of himself. But, before he was able to achieve self-appraisal, he had to complete the group of experiences which shaped his poetic vision.

A sensitivity to the changing social order is revealed in the poem "Dominus ijs opus habet," and, to Gascoigne at this point, change was closely linked with decay. In the poem, Gascoigne slashes at the materialism of the various classes of his society. He does not conceal his personal dislike or his bitterness toward the noblemen who ran off to court and city life leaving their lands unattended, or who rioted to such excess that they impoverished the tenants who worked their lands. Gascoigne feels, perhaps, in this respect, a sense of his own guilt for the excessive squandering of money he did in his youth. The poem, specifically, discusses the changing way of life on many social levels: kings and princes, dukes and barons, the country knights, and the country "louts" (peasants). The honest, fearless, openhearted days are gone: "Fewe men wyll lende a locke of heye, but for to gain a loade." On each level of life, he finds a tightening of purse strings; and he records the unrest which this new attitude breeds. He begins the list with "So kinges and princes both, have left thir halles at large,/ Their privie chambers cost enough, they cut off every charge"; then,

Dukes Earles and Barons bold, have learnt like lesson nowe, . . .
They feed them selves with delycates, and at the princes cost. . . .

Then come a litle lower, unto the contrey knight, . . .
Unto the good towne is he gone, to make his frends good cheere. . . .

Well, lowest nowe at last: let see the contrey loute,
And marke how he doth swink & sweat to bring this geare about:
                                                    (Prouty, 159-61)

The burden of providing for those who no longer help provide for themselves, either in farming or in managing, falls inevitably on the tenant farmer—"For better [that] Fermers fast than Manour houses fall." The result is an increasing poverty among the peasants: "His feastings be but few; cast whipstockes clout his shoone. . . ./ Dame Alyson his wyfe doth knowe the price of meale,/ Hir bridecakes be not halfe so bigge as she was wont to steale." Yet no one class of society is solely at fault; each comes in for its criticism, even the farmer who complains of the stinginess of his landlord: "Yea let suche pelters prate, saint *Needam* be their spede,/ We neede no text to answer them, but this, *The Lord hath nede.*" Gascoigne is not trying to reform; he is simply giving an ironic contrast between the old order and the new: "And in that noble glass I take delight to vewe/ The fashions of the wonted world, compared by the newe." He finds the new order lacking in the comparison, and there are overtones in the poem of corruption, greed, self-seeking—of a general moral breakdown. But he offers no solution, only pessimism and an almost callous acceptance.

A more bitter treatment of the state of his society is given in the poem upon the theme "Durum aeneum & miserabile aeuum":

When peerelesse Princes courtes were free from flatterie,
The Justice from Unequal doome, the quest from perjurie,
The pillers of the state from proude presumption,
The clearkes from heresie, the Commones from rebellion:
Then righte rewards were given by swaye of dewe deserte,
Then vertues derlinges might be plaste aloft to play their part:
Then might they coumpt it true that hath been sayd of olde,
The children of those happie dayes were borne in beds of golde,
And swadled in the same: . . .
But nowe the tymes are turnde, it is not as it was,
The golde is gone, the silver sunke, and nothing left but brasse.
To see a king encroache, what wonder should it seeme,
When commons cannot be content with countrie *Dyadeeme*?
The Prince maye dye a babe, trust up by trecherie,
Where vaine ambition doth move trustlesse nobilitie.
Errours in pulpit preache, where faith in preesthood failes,
Promotion (not devotion) is cause why cleargie quailes.
Thus is the stage stakt out where all these partes be plaide,
And I the prologue should pronounce, but that I am afraide.
First *Cayphas* playes the Priest, and *Herode* sits as king,
Pylate the Judge, *Judas* the Jurour, verdict in doth bring;

Vaine tatling plaies the Vice, well cladde in rich aray,
And poore Tom Troth is laught to skorn, with garments nothing gay.
(Prouty, 158)

Gascoigne's harsh comparison is made effective by the morality
play scene suggested in the last six lines quoted. It binds England to the Classical concept of the golden and brass ages through
placing symbols of the fallen age in judgment over England.

III *Personal Lyrics*

There is a discernible satiric intention in the two poems "Dominus ijs opus habet" and "Durum aeneum & miserabile aeuum"
in that the poet overtly criticizes the existing social standards.
Yet, in each poem the poet turns upon himself in an ironic
sense and makes the over-all tone of the poem one of wryness.
In "Dominus ijs opus habet," the poet injects the flavor of his
personality into the whole poem by means of the first six lines:

My recklesse race is runne, greene youth and pride be past,
My riper mellowed yeeres beginne to follow on as fast:
My glancing lookes are gone, which wonted were to prie
In everie gorgious garishe glass that glistred in mine eie.
My sight is now so dimme, it can behold none such,
No mirrour but the merrie meane can please my fansie muche.

It is an aging and vain poet who describes his world, not a
skilled and critical observer; and the poet's self-awareness is
carried through the poem by such lines as "I mocke? not I! my
text is true, beleeve it as your creed." and "Thus learn I by my
glasse that merrie meane is best." There is ironic censure throughout the poems, as in the lines:

The world is wondrous feareful now, for danger bids men doubt,
And aske how chaunceth this? or what meanes all this meede?
Forsoothe the common aunswere is, because *the Lord hath neede*.
A noble jest by gisse, I finde it in my glasse,
The same freeholde our saviour Christ conveyed to his asse.

The harshness and lack of sympathy at the end of the poem
("Yea let such pelters prate") emphasize the poet's crabbed
and selfish personality in the poem, but they also emphasize
the irrevocability of the change that has occurred and the fruit-
lessness of even wishing it away. Both the poet's world and the
poet himself have become merely material things at the poem's
conclusion, and the contrast with what once was—in the world

and in the poet—is not just a subject for irony; it is mainly a source of deep sadness. In this mood, it is quite similar to the poem discussed earlier, "Spreta tamen viuunt."

In "Durum aeneum & miserabile aeuum," the couplet which ends the poem both reinforces the criticism and turns ironically upon the poet: "And thus this foolishe jest, I put in dogrell rime,/ Bicause a crosier staffe is best, for such a crooked time." A "foolishe jest" and "dogrell rime" suggest that the poet considers his poem inane; yet that very inanity reflects the "crooked time" which he writes about and participates in.

We may reasonably argue that such poems as these could be classed as satiric rather than lyric poems, and in many ways they should be because they strongly criticize the social injustices of the time. But, at times, lyric and satire blend closely together. In these poems, we can see many lyrical elements alongside the satiric. The poet speaks more to himself than to an audience at large; the mood is not wholly ironic or cynical or bitter but is a blend of the poet's attitude toward himself as well as toward the subject matter. In his long formal satire, *The Steele Glas,* Gascoigne is always above his material—he does not inject his personality into it; and the result is that the tone is consistent, although it may vary in intensity. One of the advantages of using a Classical model, or of pretending to use one as Gascoigne does, is that the poet may remain outside his material and manipulate it to suit him, whereas normally the poet runs the danger of becoming emotionally involved. This distinction holds only for the expression, for, of course, the poet's emotions are involved in the material in both cases. But in *The Steele Glas,* the poet's voice is somewhat caustic, sometimes scolding, but always objective, aloof from the material.

The material which Gascoigne uses lends itself to this confusion of types. Running throughout his poetry is a sense of universal decay or disintegration; and, as pointed out earlier, the decaying social order is reflected in his satire and the decay of the individual in such poems as "Lullabye" and "Gascoigne's wodmanship." However, because Gascoigne links his personal successes and failures with the events that surround him, to such an extent at times that his personal fortune becomes a part of that event, we can see how the treatment of the material may be at once lyrical and satirical. Perhaps the best example of Gascoigne's use of outward events as a means to discover him-

66   GEORGE GASCOIGNE

self as an individual is the poem "Gascoigne's wodmanship," in which the outward event is the poet's lack of ability to bring down a deer. The poem contains a good share of satire, but it is predominantly lyrical work.

"Gascoigne's wodmanship" is described by Yvor Winters in *Poetry*, XIII (Oct., 1938) as one of the two or three finest lyric poems of the century; although Winters does not elaborate upon his opinion, an examination of the poem brings to light several impressive characteristics. The basic analysis of the poem shows it to be iambic pentameter, its rhyme scheme is *ababcdcdefef* and so forth, and it has no division into stanzas. The syntax is smooth and does not depend upon the rhyme. The weaknesses that we normally accuse Gascoigne of are not present to any extent in the poem. There is almost no overuse of alliteration; the two lines, "And sheare him out his share in ragged sheetes" and "And winne the meane which may the man mainteine," offer the most objectionable examples of it. Also, although his diction is blunt and pointed, it is seldom crude; instead it is concise, clear, and effective, as in this example:

> He cannot pull the spoile from such as pill
> And seeme full angrie at such foule offence,
> Although the gayne content his greedie will,
> Under the cloake of contrarie pretence:
> And now adayes, the man that shootes not so,
> May shoote amisse, even as your Woodman dothe:
> (Prouty, 181-84)

But, even though the poem has few of Gascoigne's typical weaknesses and could be considered to be "good Gascoigne," we might object that this quality alone does not make a poem great. However, Gascoigne does achieve several important poetic effects in the poem. First, he works out a complex analogy between deer hunting and his own life which includes a parable at the end, the understanding of which is based on the imagery of the opening lines. Secondly, he establishes a delicate, consistent tone in the poem, a difficult feat in that the tone from start to finish balances on a line between questioning and reluctant acceptance. The tone combines cries of injustice, feelings of reproach, moments of frustration, feelings of self-pride, and a sense of universal irony underlying the hopelessness of endless misfortune. Perhaps I should emphasize the poet's realization of his own personal worth, his self-pride; for the purpose behind the poem is to suggest the injustice of the low position of one so worthy of better things, as is the poet.

The poem opens with a description of the all-important dramatic setting, with a suggestion of the underlying analogy, and with a direct statement of it:

> My worthy Lord, I pray you wonder not
> To see your wodman shoote so ofte awrie,
> Nor that he stands amased like a sot,
> And lets the harmlesse deare (unhurt) go by.
> Or if he strike a doe which is but carren,
> Laugh not good Lord, but favoure such a fault,
> Take well in worth, he wold faine hit the barren,
> But though his harte be good, his happe is naught: . . .
> Beleeve me *L.* the case is nothing strange,
> He shootes awrie almost at every marke, . . .

A carrion doe, of course, is one that is pregnant, and is therefore unfit for eating or killing. After this opening, the poem bases its organization on the marks the poet shot at and missed: law, the court, and soldiering. In each he strove to be a success; but he failed in each because with the law:

> . . . he most mislikte the thing
> Which most might helpe to guide the arrow streight,
> He winked wrong, and so let slippe the string,
> Which cast him wide, for all his queint conceit.

with the court:

> Yet more than them, the marks of dignitie,
> He much mistooke and shot the wringer way,
> Thinking the purse of prodigalitie,
> Had bene best meane to purchase such a prey.

and with soldiering, for he was too kindhearted to become wealthy by pillaging, cheating, or extortion.

The poem then turns to a defense of the poet:

> Yet therewithall I can not but confesse,
> That vayne presumption makes my heart to swell,
> For thus I thinke, not all the worlde (I guesse,)
> Shootes bet than I, nay some shootes not so well.

But, even though taught by Aristotle, Tully, Parkyns, John Rastall, and Bracton, he cannot escape the irony of his life:

Yet can not these with manye maystries mo,
Make me shoote streyght at any gaynfull pricke,
Where some than never handled such a bow,
Can hit the white, or touch it neare the quicke,
Who can nor speake, nor write in pleasant wise,
Nor leade their life by *Aristotles* rule,
Nor argue well on questions that arise,
Nor pleade a case more than my Lord Maiors mule,
Yet can they hit the marks that I do misse,
And winne the meane which may the man mainteine,
Nowe when my mynde dothe mumble upon this,
No wonder then although I pyne for payne:
And whyles myne eyes beholde this mirroure thus,
The hearde goeth by, and farewell gentle does: . . .

The pathos in the last line establishes the tone of the poem
with finality. The analogy of the gentle does and the successful
life is plain, and the poet's farewell to them is doubly poignant,
for he sees in their passing the end of all chances to achieve
success. And again, the irony is not that he is a poor marks-
man, but that he shot at the wrong marks, and that, when he
finally gains this wisdom, he is too old to do it over again. The
term "mark" has a double meaning on the figurative level, being
both the immediate end—for example, successful courtier—and
the abstract end, success in life.

The short parable at the end is an unusual technique of summing up a poem:

Let me imagine in this woorthlesse verse:
If right before mee, at my standings foote
There stoode a Doe, and I should strike hir deade,
And then shee prove a carrion carkas too,
What figure might I fynde within my head,
To scuse the rage whiche rulde mee so to doo?
Some myghte interprete by playne paraphrase,
That lacke of skill or fortune ledde the chaunce,
But I muste otherwyse expounde the case,
I saye *Jehova* did this Doe advaunce,
And made hir bolde to stande before mee so,
Till I had thrust myne arrowe to hir harte,
That by the sodaine of hir overthrowe,
I myght endevour to amende my parte,
And turne myne eyes that they no more beholde,
Suche guylefull markes as seeme more than they be:
And though they glister outwardely lyke golde,

Are inwardly but brasse, as men may see:
And when I see the milke hang in hir teate,
Me thinkes it sayth, olde babe now learne to sucke,
Who in thy youthe couldst never learne the feate
To hitte the whytes whiche live with all good lucke.
Thus have I tolde my Lorde, (God graunt in season)
A tedious tale in rime, but little reason.

This conclusion is organic to the poem both structurally and
thematically. Structurally, it reinforces the analogy between the
poet's life and the shooting of deer. It reiterates the carrion
doe image of the poem's opening, here supplying it with the
overt meaning that was only suggested in its first use; the carrion doe is the outstanding symbol of the poem, standing for
the uselessness of all parts of the poet's past life. Thematically,
it clarifies the poet's position. The poet is to suck at the carrion
doe's teat, thereby himself becoming all that she stands for—
something wasted and unwanted! Also, the parable makes clear
that ill luck is not involved. Rather, Jehovah, or God, sent the
doe to teach the poet his lesson; that is, each failure of the poet
is meant to tell him that success in the eyes of the world is not
his fate. He must learn to accept his futile life—nothing more.
These final lines are indispensable to the completeness of the
poem.

Within the poem are a few attempts to justify the poet's
failures, particularly when he was a soldier; and there is even
an appeal for help when the poet says he will remain poor
"unlesse your lordship deigne,/ To traine him yet into some
better trade." Yet, the poem stands as a strong complex statement of a man's appraisal of his own life. In its content, in its
self-awareness and honesty, it is almost unique; in its complexity
it has unity and meaning. There is little sweetness of expression,
but the diction is clear, forceful, and restrained, and every detail
the poet uses forwards the purpose of the poem.

IV *The Religious Lyric*

If, as suggested, the pessimistic tone of Gascoigne's poetry
had its foundations in the social and moral evils and in the
personal decay and death which he saw around him, he must
have felt very little personal stability or security in the everyday
world; for kingdoms, fortunes, high positions, and reputations
were continually being broken down and ruined. All that awaited

any individual were death and the grave. Overtones of this
feeling crept into many of his lyrics, as has already been pointed
out. But, in three of the poems, he faces the problem of death
directly and tries to find a solution to it. Wavering as he does
between a type of stoical philosophy and an essentially Christian ethic, his solution is not original. In much of his lyric
poetry, he establishes the certainty of corruption, decay, and
death; and, as in "Lullabye," he does not know quite how to
handle it beyond simple acceptance. However, in the poems
"Gascoignes good nyghte," "Gascoignes good morrow," and
"Gascoignes De profundis," which we shall briefly examine,
he accepts the orthodox Christian attitude that the terrors of
the grave can be overcome by a belief in God. He faces the certainty and the horror of the grave and decides that the only
escape is through the intervention of God.

In all of Gascoigne's poems, there is a remarkable concern
for things of the world and of the flesh. He worries over success
in worldly affairs, success in love, and the state of his body.
Occasionally, he writes to prove in poetry the truth of a statement, as in the poem upon the theme *Satis sufficit* in which he
supports the idea that neither excessive wealth nor excessive
poverty is a satisfactory state, but that the best life lies somewhere in between. Yet even in this poem, although the purpose
is to establish an abstract truth, the examples deal with fleshly
and material appetites. In the three poems just named, Gascoigne
does not mention hell or evil; instead, he is concerned with the
loss of conscious life and with the decay of the body. He looks
on death simply as darkness, and the horrors of death are not
the Old Testament ones of hell but those of the grave. In Dan
Bartholomew's "Last will and Testament" he says: "Then I
bequeath my corps to couche beneath hir bones,/ And there
to feede the greedie woorms that linger for the nones/ To
frette upon hir fleshe, which is too fyne therefore,..." (Prouty,
215). In the "good nyghte," he says:

My bed it self is lyke ye grave, my sheetes ye winding sheete,
My clothes the moulde which I must have to cover me most meet:
The hungrie fleas which friske so fresh, to worms I can compare,
Which greedily shal gnaw my flesh, and leave the bones ful bare: ...
                                                        (Prouty, 164)

In his "good morrow" darkness and sleep are equated with death,
and it is they which fill him with horror:

> The dreadfull night with darkesome stormes
> Had overspread the lyght,
> And sluggishe sleepe with drowsynesse,
> Had overpreste our myght:
> A glasse wherein we may beholde
> Eche storme that stoppes our breath,
> Our bedde the grave, oure cloathes lyke molde,
> And sleepe lyke dreadfull death.

> (Prouty, 162)

In none of these instances does Gascoigne suggest damnation, although he does mention purgatory in the "Last will and Testament" as an afterthought. The thought of bodily decay is horror enough; sufficient retribution for sins is found in just the specter of death.

If Gascoigne does not have a clear idea of what sort of punishment to expect, he does at least know what may cause such punishment, and he lists some things in "good nyghte." First, if one's conscience bothers him, he should ask for mercy in his nighttime prayers. Second, he should admit humbly that God, not himself, is responsible for all the good of the preceding day— that is, he should not be proud. Third, he should not be lustful. Fourth, he should not be slothful. Although Gascoigne does not enumerate the seven deadly sins, he certainly has them in mind.

Gascoigne's concept of salvation in these poems appears to be a simplified version of the one given in Revelations:

> The daye is lyke the daye of doome,
> The sunne, the Sonne of man,
> The skyes the heavens, the earth the toombe
> Wherein we reste till than.

> The Raynbowe bending in the skye, . . .
> Is lyke the seate of God on hye, . . .
> So by the bloud whiche Christe hath shead,
> He will oure health restore.

> (Prouty, 162-63)

Yet, damnation and salvation are still presented as the simple contrasts between day and night, or light and darkness:

> And sende us after worldly payne,
> In heaven to have a place.
> Where wee may still enjoy that lyght,
> Whiche never shall decay:

> (Prouty, 163)

and: "And as I ryse up lustily, when sluggishe sleepe is paste,/
So hope I to ryse joyfully, to Judgement at the laste" (Prouty,
164). For Gascoigne, the analogy between sleep and death is
not a good one because sleep gives rest and ease, quite unlike
death. He is unable to take the additional step that Hamlet does
when he soliloquizes, "To sleep? Perchance to dream! Ay, there's
the rub;/ For in that sleep of death what dreams may come,/
When we have shufff'd off this cortal coil,/ Must give us pause."
Gascoigne's hell lies in the very real disintegration of his own
body and in the parallel moral decay and corruption of the
social and economic world around him. He does not need to
dream, to borrow horrors. The devil is, for him, simply a crow
flying about doing evil to live people:

> The carrion Crowe, that lothesome beast,
> Whyche cryes agaynst the rayne,
> Bothe for hir hew and for the reste,
> The Devill resembleth playne:
>   (Prouty, 163)

The most perfect state for Gascoigne is youth; heaven could
only be a prolongation of that period. He has no deep philosophic insight into religious problems. He knows only the
material, earthy characteristics of humans—their pleasures, passions, and pains. He does not concern himself overly with man's
soul. The terms of salvation which he reaches in the two poems
discussed, and reflects in "De profundis," are simply that man
must place all faith in God.

V Conclusion

When we scan the whole body of Gascoigne's lyric poetry to
determine what is and what is not valuable, the first quality that
strikes us is the intensely personal character of the poetry. The
poems are the subjective record of emotions, of feelings, and
of reactions to the surrounding world. For the most part, Gascoigne makes himself the subect of his poems, and we see him
in a variety of attitudes—examining his relations with ladies
of the court, his loss of youth and subsequent loss of attractiveness, his failures, his fear of dying, and so forth. At other times,
he writes of his reaction to the changing society around him.
In either instance, the poet is recognizable behind the poem;
he is not obscured by it, partly because he seldom relies on

artificial conventions. His lyric poetry is an extension of himself, of all parts of his personality, and is not bland or impersonal as is so much of the contemporary poetry.

A second quality of Gascoigne's poetry is its variety. In its subject matter, its mood, its verse form, and its technique, it achieves great breadth of applicability and effect. The subject matter includes many aspects of love; it includes social criticism and self-analysis. Its approach is philosophic, religious, mock-serious, and didactic. His poetry enters nearly all fields and experiments with nearly all kinds of verse form. His mood varies from tenderness to harsh cynicism, but the emphasis is on pessimism.

Finally, the question of whether all this poetry is or is not good boils down to poetic technique; and we have found that, when Gascoigne borrows the technique of the Petrarchan imitators, his poetry is usually poor. But most of the poems which do not imitate are successful; some, excellent. Gascoigne usually writes to discover or establish a truth in poetry. That truth may vary from showing the validity of an old Latin proverb to precisely delineating the position of a certain lover in his quest for satisfaction. To establish truth, he uses proverbs, examples, similes, metaphors, analogies—in short, the usual poetical or rhetorical figures. Upon occasion he uses a symbol. When the truth is established, or proven, the success of the poem usually depends on the depth or sophistication of the particular truth. But, when the truth is reinforced by the mood of the poem, however created, either through diction as in "Lullabye" or through poetical figures as in "Gascoignes wodmanship," so that the content and the mood interact and cause tension or irony to result, the poem can approach brilliance, as these two poems do.

Thus, to answer satisfactorily the question of Gascoigne's ability as a poet, we can say at least that the following qualities of his verse are valuable: the variety of his verse form and content; the accuracy of his social and psychological perception; the control of tone he exhibits in his lighter poems such as "Gascoignes recantation" and "Gascoignes araignement"; and his departure from the tradition of Petrarch.

CHAPTER 5

Style and War:
Aspects of the Poetic Mind

BURIED somewhere within the work of every poet lie the basic formative principles upon which his poetry is constructed. With some poets, such as Spenser and Sidney, such principles are difficult to isolate. With others, such as Lyly, Drayton, perhaps Lodge, we find them more easily in the principles of rhetoric and in the basic diction of the Petrarchists. Chapman, Ben Jonson, and Shakespeare, in their plays, conversations, and various critical writings, have left records of how they believed poetry should be written; and their comments, although often confusing and contradictory when applied to their own works, are of immense value in understanding the principles at work in the poetry of the period.

Gascoigne is one of the rare poets who not only formulated a working set of principles for the writing of poetry but also followed them to a large extent. As it can be cogently argued that Gascoigne holds a key position in a continuing line of poetic development, the analysis of his poetry in the light of his own stated principles becomes important. This chapter attempts to show what those principles are and, to some extent, how they affected his poetry. One immediate result of his poetic theories was that his poetry quickly became considered out of date, an attitude framed in a Gabriel Harvey epigram: "Yet this new fangled youth, made for these times/ Doth, above all, praise old George Gascoigne's rhymes." But, in spite of the fact that his critics were partly right when they complained that his poetry was harsh and unmusical, Gascoigne's diction and style were the direct cause of several valuable qualities in his poetry as well.

I *"Certayne notes of Instruction"*

In "The Epistle to the reverend Divines," which prefaces the edition of 1575, Gascoigne suggests that he is a poet in the

English tradition, a concern which indicates an awareness of a fading tradition: "Next unto this, I have alwayes bene of opinion, that it is not unpossible eyther in Poemes or in Prose too write both compendiously and perfectly in our Englishe tongue. And therefore although I chalenge not unto my selfe the name of an English Poet, yet may the Reader finde oute in my wrytings, that I have more faulted in keeping the olde English wordes (*quamuis iam obsoleta*) than in borrowing of other languages such Epithetes and Adiectives as smell of the Inkhorne." (Cunliffe, I, 5).

As did John Cheke, Roger Ascham, and others, Gascoigne defends the propriety of the English language as a vehicle for poetry. He rejects the popular practice of coining new word combinations suggested by other languages, or of borrowing words directly from foreign vocabularies, in particular from Latin, French, and Greek; rather, he insists on the capability of the English vocabulary to supply all the needed words, even though he is often forced into using words "*quamuis iam obsoleta*" to satisfy his verse. However, he realizes that he may be forced into a practice which he dislikes, so he qualifies his position further on in the letter, in another reference to the controversy over English poetic diction: "To the seconde, although I be sometimes constreyned for the cadence or rimes, or *per licentiam Poeticam,* to use an inkehorne terme or a straunge word: yet hope I that it shall be apparant I have rather regarde to make our language commendable in it selfe, than gay with the feathers of straunge birdes" (Cunliffe, I, 6). These quotations tell us that Gascoigne had established a working theory of poetic diction, that he had put it into operation, and that he realized that it contained certain imperfections which he simply accepted.

But, in spite of his apology, Gascoigne's poetry does not abound with archaic words. He does use old forms of English verbs, much in the way that Spenser uses them; but they stand out as much from their infrequency as from their strangeness. *The Steele Glas* contains a number of archaic forms, but they are used to enhance the over-all medieval flavor of the poem. His other poems contain such old forms as "withouten," "ysojorned," "yfraught," "foughten," and such archaic words as "gatt" (got), "moyling" (defiling one's self), "coone" (apparently, to give; not found in the *Oxford English Dictionary*), and "gite" (gown), words not commonly used that satisfy Gascoigne's requirement for Anglo-Saxon and English monosyllabic words.

Occasionally, Gascoigne was not above using an "inkhornism." His use of "recomforte" and "recure" shows how he tried to make new words by juggling roots and prefixes; although these examples have died out of the language—"recomforte" is replaced by "discomfort," and "recure" by "reheal"—he uses many which have remained current. Another "inkhorn" quality is the use of foreign words directly in English. In an example from "The Fruit of Fetters," he uses "fine," meaning "end," because it fits the needs of his alliteration and rhyme when given an English pronunciation:

> And since the storye is both new and trew,
> A dreary tale much like these lottes of myne,
> I will assaye my muse for to renewe,
> By ryming out his frowarde fatall fine.
>   (Cunliffe, I, 369)

The essential character of Gascoigne's diction is his use of monosyllabic words. As we may observe in "Epistle to the reverend Divines," he consciously stays away from polysyllabic coinages or borrowings, words which "smell of the inkhorne." His loyalty to his native tongue forces him to exhort the priests in *The Steele Glas* to pray for "Cantabridge":

> That *Grammer* grudge not at our english tong,
> Bycause it stands by *Monosyllaba,*
> And cannot be declined as others are.
> Pray thus (my priests) for universities.
>   (Cunliffe, II, 169)

The emphasis he places on monosyllables is significant. In note five of "Certayne notes of Instruction," he cautions Master Edouardo Donati:

Here by the way I thinke it not amisse to forewarne you that you thrust as few wordes of many syllables into your verse as may be: and hereunto I might alledge many reasons: first, the more monasyllables that you use, the truer Englishman you shall seeme, and the lesse you shall smell of the Inkhorne. Also wordes of many syllables to cloye a verse and make it unpleasant, whereas woordes of one syllable will more easily fall to be shorte or long as occasion requireth, or wilbe adapted to become circumflexe or of an indifferent sounde.   (Cunliffe, I, 468-69)

In this instruction, we find two important points that ruled much of Gascoigne's poetical composition. The first, "so that the more monasyllables that you use, the truer Englishman you shall seeme," indicates his strong desire to give his poetry a national character. This desire shows a motivating force behind much of his diction: the belief that monosyllabic words reflect the Anglo-Saxon part of his language's heritage. The other point is a more practical one: "woordes of many syllables do cloye a verse and make it unpleasant." The thought flows more freely, and the verse is more elastic when one-syllable words are used; for they do not overload the line, either with sounds or with imageless abstractions.

Gascoigne remained faithful to this particular instruction, and much of what is both very good and very bad in his poetry is directly attributable to his concept of diction. Much of the harshness, the repetition, and the prosaic quality of his poetry—most of the qualities to which Gabriel Harvey, Sir John Davies, and Drayton objected—arise almost exclusively from his choice of words. For example, in "Gascoignes De profundis," he begins one stanza:

> O Israell, O householde of the Lorde,
> O *Abrahams* Brattes, O broode of blessed seede,
> O chosen sheepe that love the Lord in deede:
> O hungrye heartes, feede styll upon his worde,
> And put your trust in him with one accorde.
>   (Cunliffe, I, 61)

The harshness of the word "Brattes" intrudes upon the sublimity of the subject matter and even suggests the language of the streets in what otherwise is an impassioned plea for faith and trust in God; and we wonder why the poet has the offensive word followed immediately by the poetically good word, "broode."

Another word, "grutch," is impressive in its utter lack of music, even in these lines of bad poetry: "Thou knowst I honored hir no more, but all too much,/ Alas, thou knowst she cast me off, when I deservde no grutch." (Cunliffe, I, 371); and in:

> These things seeme strange, yit ar they trew
> Beleeve me, sweete, my state is such:
> One pleasure which I would eschew,
> Both slakes my grief, and breedes my grutch.
>   (Prouty, 127)

"Grutch," "dole," "bale," "dread of dark annoye," and "drop of
dark disdain" are words and phrases which Gascoigne, for what
he evidently thought was their mood-evoking power, uses over
and over. In the majority of instances, they occur in those poems
which deal with the pangs of love. Their regular occurrence has
the effect of a refrain; and, although they do not jar our poetic
sensibilities, they do reduce our enjoyment of the sound of the
poems in which they occur.

Gascoigne's theory of poetic diction, then, has its foundations
in a respect for the traditional English vocabulary; and his
practice is an attempt to retain it. To do so, he uses many monosyllabic words; and he occasionally uses Old English prefixes
and case endings. However, this practice creates certain problems for the modern reader; for in the attempt to utilize the
Anglo-Saxon vocabulary, he often chooses a word offensive to
the modern ear. Frequently, because of the limited number of
words to choose from, he is forced to use certain words many
times, with the result that they lose their poetic effectiveness
because of monotonous repetition. For the same reason, he uses
obsolete words and forms. It cannot be fairly said, however,
that his use of obsolete words is disruptive to our enjoyment
of the poems, for he uses them generally only where the rhyme
or the meter demand them; hence, they present themselves to
our ear unobtrusively, and we tend to accept them uncritically.
Finally, Gascoigne's theory does allow him some leeway in
using foreign or newly coined words, and he justifies their
usage in a purely practical sense by pointing out that strange
words often draw attention to themselves, thereby heightening
their poetic effect.

II *Pleasure and Truth*

Aside from his diction, a major reason for the singular lack
of success of his court poetry lies in his use of Classical literature
and mythology. Influenced obviously by the translations and
imitations around him, and to a large extent by Chaucer's
adaptation of the Italian, he used foreign literary allusions in a
large number of his poems. As a result, the inherent purpose of
his poetry—to reveal truth—is at times smothered by his adventi-
tious desire to heighten his verse with foreign references.

By far his most repeated allusion is to the story of Troilus and
Cressida; the inherent moral in the story satisfies his somewhat

critical attitude toward woman, and he uses the names at times almost as adjectives:

> For *Cressyde* fayre did *Troylus* never love,
> More deare than I esteemd your framed cheare: ...
>   (Prouty, 140)

> Yes God he knowes, for verse nor pleasaunt rymes,
> Can constant keepe, the key of Cressides crimes. ...
>   (Prouty, 142)

> In colder cares are my conceipts consumd,
> Than *Dido* felt when false *Enaes* fled:
> In farre more heat, than trusty *Troylus* fumd,
> When craftie *Cressyde* dwelt with *Diomed*.
>   (Prouty, 143)

The reference is usually to her inconstancy or to her duping of Troylus, and he uses it when he points out some flaw in a woman. Other frequent references are to Helen and Paris, and to the various Olympian gods and goddesses. He uses Classical literature and mythology in several ways. The least effective but the most frequent way is to decorate his verse. A second way is to prove a point. Another is to praise a woman, and the final way is to retell a story in order to point out a moral.

When Gascoigne uses Classical allusions to embellish his poetry, they usually intrude upon the poetic effect of the poem. Frequently, they serve as little more than padding; at times, they appear absurd in relation to the rest of the poem. In the poem written on the theme *Spreta tamen viuunt,* the padding effect can be seen as the poet complains of losing his loved one to another:

I am now set full light, who earst was dearely lov'd:
Som newfound choyce is more esteemd, than y^t which wel was prov'd.
Some *Diomede* is crept into Dame *Cressydes* hart:
And trustie Troylus now is taught in vayne to playne his part.
                          (Prouty, 126)

In this example, the fact of lost love is simply reiterated, adding nothing essential to the poem. In the poem upon the theme *Satis sufficit,* Gascoigne develops the point that the contented man is he who has neither too much nor too little. Much of the poem is developed by proverbs of a distinctly English flavor:

If so thy wyfe be too too fayre of face,
It drawes one guest (too manie) to thyne inne:
If she be fowle, and foyled with disgrace,
In other pillowes prickst thou many a pinne:
So fowle prove fooles, and fayrer fall to sinne.
Wherefore to lacke the moste, and leave the least,
I coumpte enough as good as any feast.
                              (Prouty, 153-54)

But placed among these proverbs is an example drawn from mythology:

By too too much *Dan Croesus* caught his death,
And bought with bloud the price of glittering gold,
By too too litle many one lacks breath
And sterves in streetes a mirroure to behold:
So pride for heate, and povert pynes for colde.

This allusion to a foreign literature disrupts the unity of the poem and even affects the tone: although the example is short, it has an air of sophistication that sets it apart from the other, more earthy examples. It has another effect which Gascoigne did not consider. Except for this allusion, the poem uses wisdom drawn from real life experiences; the mythological example is unreal, is a moral lesson by itself, and does not allow any additional lesson to be drawn from it. For two reasons, then, the allusion hurts the poem.

It is interesting to note that most of Gascoigne's best lyric poems are free from such devices—"Gascoignes wodmanship," "Gascoignes good nyght," and "Lullabye of a lover"; and, in the better poems that do have some use of them, they are employed sparingly and are integrated into the poem. Thus, in the poem "Dominus ijs opus habet," only one line is so afflicted: "*Jove, Mars,* and *Mercurie,* Dame *Venus* and the rest,/ They banquet not as they were wont, they know it were not best" (Prouty, 160). The example it establishes is further evidence of the increasing stinginess of the world, and it rightly satisfies that part of the poem which deals with "our onely God," "the heathens Gods," and the Classical ones. The apparent conclusion that can be drawn is that when Gascoigne used Classical and mythological allusions simply for decoration, the poem was unsuccessful. He did not write the graceful, rich poetry that allowed such embellishments; since his poetry was harsher,

more devoted to truth than to sweetness of effect, the less
decoration he used, the more effective was the poem.

Certain interesting conclusions can be drawn when we contrast Gascoigne's handling of Classical and mythological material
to that of a later poet such as Christopher Marlowe. The contrast was recognized by such men as Drayton, who certainly had
in mind the more decorated and figure-laden poetry of the
later poets when he regarded Gascoigne's poetry as rude and out
of date. Certainly to the late-century critics, the richer the
diction was, the softer the sound; and the more melodious the
verse was, then the better the poem. In view of the fact that one
of the achievements of High Renaissance poetry was to link
Classical subject matter and style with English forms of expression, we can see why Classical and mythological allusions,
sweetly descriptive words, and polysyllabic, often abstract diction became some of the outstanding characteristics of the
period's poetry. The purpose of poetry had changed, and in
the following examples from Marlowe's *Hero and Leander*, we
can see the grace and beauty that can be achieved by these new
tools. Marlowe describes Hero's garments as follows:

> The outside of her garments were of lawne,
> The lining purple silde, with guilt starres drawne,
> Her wide sleeves greene, and bordered with a grove,
> Where *Venus* in her naked glosy strove,
> To please the carelesse and disdainful eies
> Of proud *Adonis* that before her lies.
> Her kirtle blew, whereon was many a staine.
> Upon her head she ware a myrtle wreath,
> From whence her vaile reacht to the ground beneath.
> Her vaile was artificiall flowers and leaves,
> Whose workmanship both man and beast deceaves.[1]

In this example, Marlowe combines mythology with descriptive
hyperbole to create the impression of a reality just beyond man's
experience. In describing Hero herself, Marlowe relinquishes
physical description and concentrates on expressing her beauty
by showing her effect on various mythological entities, a per-
suasive technique rather than a descriptive one:

> At *Sestos*, Hero Dwelt; *Hero* the fair,
> Whom young *Apollo* courted for her haire,
> And offred as a dower his burning throne,
> Where she should sit for men to gaze upon. . . .

Some say, for her the fairest *Cupid* pyn'd,
And looking in her face, was strooken blind.
But this is true, so like was one the other,
As he imagyn'd *Hero* was his mother.
And oftentimes into her bosome flew,
About her naked necke his bare armes threw,
And laid his childish head upon her brest,
And with still panting rockt, there tooke his rest.
So lovely faire was *Hero, Venus* Nun,
As nature wept, thinking she was undone;
Because she tooke more from her than she left,
Therefore in signe her treasure suffred wracke,
Since *Heroes* time, hath halfe the world beene blacke.[2]

The effect of such description is to create a sensual experience
for the reader. The use of such words as "naked," "bare,"
"bosome," "brest," "panting," and so forth establishes the mood
for erotic sections further on in the poem; it suggests additional
sensual experiences for the reader if he continues reading the
poem, and Marlowe's artistry is such that the reader achieves
sensual gratification. In the final seduction scene, Marlowe's half-
cynical, half-humorous tone allows him to write an excellent
piece of erotic poetry:

Yet ever as he greedily assayd
To touch those dainties, she the *Harpey* playd,
And every lim did as a soldier stout,
Defend the fort, and keep the foe-man out.
For though the rising yu'rie mount he scal'd
Which is with azure circling lines empal'd,
Much like a globe, (a globe may I tearme this,
By which love sailes to regions full of blis,)
Yet there with *Sysiphus* he toyld in vaine,
Till gentle parlie did the truce obtaine.
Wherein *Leander* on her quivering brest,
Breathlesse spoke some thing, and sigh'd out the rest;
Which so prevail'd, as he with small ado
Inclos'd her in his armes and kist her to.
And everie kisse to her was a charme,
And to *Leander* as a fresh alarme,
So that the truce was broke, and she alas,
(Poore sillie maiden) at his mercie was.
Love is not ful of pittie (as men say)
But deaffe and cruell, where he means to pray.
Even as a bird, which in our hands we wring,

> She trembling strove, this strife of hers (like that
> Which made the world) another world begat
> Of unknowne joy. Treason was in her thought,
> And cunningly to yeeld her selfe she sought.
> Seeming not woon, yet woon she was at length,
> In such warres women use but halfe their strength.
> *Leander* now like Theban *Hercules,*
> Entred the orchard of *Th'esperides,*
> Whose fruit none rightly can describe but hee
> That puls or shakes it from the golden tree:
> And now she wisht this night were never done,
> And sigh'd to thinke upon th'approching sunne,
> For much it greev'd her that the bright day-light
> Should know the pleasure of this blessed night,
> And them like *Mars* and *Ericine* display,
> Both in each others armes chaind as they lay.[3]

Marlowe, who dangles his images before the reader, suggests through allusions what happens rather than giving outright description. He mingles suggestions of cruelty and lust with the sensuality by mentioning wringing the neck of a bird—an interesting symbol of the loss of innocence, and the closest approach to realistic description which Marlowe allows himself.

The rudeness of Gascoigne's verse, perhaps even the justification of Sir John Davies's epithet "old-fashioned," can be seen in comparison with the above lines. When Gascoigne describes the heroine of his mytho-erotic poem, "The Complaint of Philomene," he simply says:

> Faire *Phylomene* came forth
> In comely garments cladde,
> As one whom newes of sisters helth
> Had moved to be gladde,...
> (Cunliffe, II, 184)

Describing her attractiveness to Tereus, he says:

> Wherewith he fixt his eyes
> Uppon hir fearefull face.
> And stil behelde hir gestures all,
> And all hir gleames of grace.
> (Cunliffe, II, 187))

There is nothing sweet or pleasing in these verses. They are direct and to the point of the narrative; nothing distracts the reader from the over-all story. When the seduction occurs, it is brutal and unsavory:

> And al alone (alone)
> With force he hir supprest,
> And made hir yelde the wicked weede
> Whose flowre he liked best.
> (Cunliffe, II, 187)

When Philomene threatens to spread the tale of the rape, Tereus cuts out her tongue. Gascoigne continues:

> I blush to tell this tale,
> But sure best books say this:
> That yet the butcher did not blush
> Hir bloudy mouth to kisse.

> And ofte hir bulke embrast,
> And ofter quencht the fire,
> Which kindled had the furnace first,
> Within his foule desire.
> (Cunliffe, II, 191)

Gascoigne, in these lines, avoids all verbal decoration; he uses the barest of adjectives and seldom displays flashes of wit, as does Marlowe. There are few lines in "The Complaint" which the reader can enjoy by themselves, but many parts of *Hero and Leander* may be enjoyably read separately.

Perhaps the greatest difference between the two poets is that Marlowe is writing on two planes of existence, the actual world and the mythological; he weaves the two together into an intricate pattern of fantasy and reality. And because his subject matter is of first love, which by its nature touches upon the fanciful, Marlowe is highly successful. Gascoigne writes strictly of the world of reality; his attention is focused on the sequence of events and on retribution for moral crimes. The magical apparatus he uses at the end—the "heavenly benche" turning Tereus into a lapwing, Progne into a swallow, Philomene into a nightingale, and the son into a cock pheasant—is simply to help him create the effect of poetic justice being meted out to all sides, as well as being faithful to the old story. At no time in the poem does Gascoigne use mythological apparatus merely as decoration for his poetry.

One of Gascoigne's purposes in the poem is to show that guilt cannot be laid to any one person. Several types of crimes have been committed; and, in reading the denouement of the poem, we are reminded again of the seven deadly sins. Tereus is guilty of lust and infidelity, almost of incest. Progne and Philomene are guilty of pride and lust for vengeance. Some very telling irony appears in Gascoigne's comments on Philomene's feelings at the punishment of Tereus, and it shows that he has grasped his subject completely:

> Phy on thy sisters facte,
> And phy hir selfe doth sing,
> Whose lack of tong nere toucht hir so
> As when it could not sting.
>   (Cunliffe, II, 201)

That is, Philomene felt her wound most keenly when, because of it, she could not give pain to another.

Just how old-fashioned Gascoigne appeared to be can be better understood when we realize that both stories are mythological tragedies. Gascoigne ostensibly tells the story of the nightingale's song, as related to him by the goddess Nemesis; but the heavily moral treatment of the story leaves little to delight the reader, and we are more concerned with what happens in the final scene than we are with nearly all the preceding ones. Compared to Marlowe's, Gascoigne's narrative technique is clumsy: a squire first hears the nightingale on a spring evening and interprets her song in a very English manner. Then the squire has a dream in which Nemesis tells him the story of Philomene and interprets the nightingale's notes—"tereu," "fy," "jug," and the strange note "nemesis"—in a different manner. The story is handled very much as a medieval dream allegory, and it presents a curious and not too successful blend of two distinct literary traditions. Marlowe's approach to the story is light and deft. The ease of his narrative style is exhibited in his opening lines:

> On Hellespont, guilty of true love's blood,
> In view and opposite two cities stood,
> Sea-borderers, disjoin'd by Neptune's might;
> The one Abydos, the other Sestos hight.
> At Sestos Hero dwelt; Hero the fair,

He begins the story simply and directly, and he fully develops each scene, blending sensuous description and satiric wit with an abundance of Classical and mythological allusions.

A comparison of *Hero and Leander* to "The Complaint of Philomene" emphasizes, however, the distinctly English characteristics of Gascoigne's handling of the mythological story. His purpose is to instruct rather than to please; therefore, he is interested more in the psychology of guilt than in that of pleasure. He uses a medieval form in which to present the story, and his diction is barren of mythological allusions beyond those few necessary for telling the story. It is easy to see how Gascoigne's poetry fell from favor. As the newer poets became skilled in using the vocabulary and wealth of allusion which the foreign literatures opened to them, the purpose and technique of their poetry changed, became richer, more decorative and sophisticated, and became more concerned with giving pleasure than with finding truth.

The weaknesses that late sixteenth-century critics found in Gascoigne's poetry spring from his theory of diction and from the purpose of his poetry. His theory of diction was to avoid foreign words and phrases and to retain the English flavor by using monosyllabic and at times archaic words. This theory precludes highly decorative and oversweet verse, but it does not rule out smoothness of line and a controlled sweetness of expression, as we find in the following lines from the introduction to "Philomene":

> In sweet April, the messenger to May
> When hoonie drops, do melt in golden showres,
> When every byrde, records hir lovers lay,
> And westerne windes do foster forth our floures,
> Late in an even, I walked out alone,
> To heare the descant of the Nightingale, . . .
>   (Cunliffe, II, 178)

These are lines of good poetry; in them can be seen the reflection of English poetry back through Surrey to Chaucer. Rather than simply marking time until the arrival of Spenser, Gascoigne and other poets like him were developing and strengthening traditional English poetry through their use of proverbs, anecdotes, nature and folklore, and plain statement. And in their development of irony and paradox, they provided an easy bridge between the poetry of Wyatt and the poetry of Donne.

III   *Three Poems of Warfare*

Three of Gascoigne's long poems concerning soldiering may serve to show some of the rewards resulting from his poetic theories. Each of them contains examples of effective diction, and each poem says something different about the life of a soldier. The purpose of all Gascoigne's poetry is to present a glimpse of truth or reality to the reader, and his diction is an essential part of that purpose; but an additional effect, perhaps unforeseen, is that his poetry conveys a strong impression of his personality, so that we become closely acquainted with him and his world. But this effect does result from his purpose; for truth and reality depend upon point of view; and, if we understand one's point of view, if we perceive the reality that he does, then we must be in sympathy with the mind that gave us that glimpse. The following poems allow us to understand one part of Gascoigne's life but, at the same time, exhibit certain aspects of his diction.

We can find examples of the vigor and movement of his poetry in sections of "Gascoignes devise of a maske," which he wrote for Viscount Mountacute as part of a wedding ceremony. In it, he recounts the trials of an English boy who, separated from his family, witnesses several battles as he struggles to return to England:

The christian crew came on, in forme of battaile pight,
And like a cressent cast them selves preparing for to fight.
On other side the Turkes, which trusted power to much,
Disorderly did spread their force, the will of God was such.
Well, at the last they met, and first with cannons thunder,
Each other sought with furious force to slit their ships in sunder.
The Barkes are battered sore, the gallies gald with shot,
The hulks are hit and every man must stand unto his lot.
The powder sendes his smoke into the cruddy skies,
The smoulder stops our nose with stench, the sunne offends our eies,
The pots of lime unsleakt, from highest top are cast,
The parched peas are not forgot to make them slip as fast.
The wilde fire works are wrought and cast in foemens face,
The grappling hooks are stretched foorth, yᵉ pikes are pusht apace.
The halberts hew on hed, the browne bills bruze the bones,
The harquebush doth spit his spight, with pretty percing stones.
The drummes crie dub a dub, the braying trumpets blow,
The whistling fifes are seldome herd, these sounds do drowne them so.
The voice of warlike wights, to comforte them that faint,
The piteous plaints of golden harts, which wer wᵗ fears attaint.
The groning of such ghosts as gasped now for breath,
The praiers of the better sort, prepared unto death,
And to be short, each griefe which on the earth may growe,

Was eath and easie to be found, uppon these flouds to flowe.
If any sight on earth, may unto hell resemble,
Then sure this was a hellishe sight, it makes me yet to tremble: . . .
(Prouty, 176-77)

It is difficult to find a battle described more realistically in
the century's verse. To find a prose description to equal it, we
would have to go to Thomas Nashe's *Unfortunate Traveller* or to
Gascoigne's *The Spoyle of Antwerpe*. The poem describes the
raw force and cruelty; the terror; and the sights, sounds, and
smells of hand-to-hand warfare as seen through the eyes of an
inexperienced youth whose mind has vividly recorded the scenes
and has brought to them the excitement and colorful bravado
which all youths feel toward warfare.

The poem "Gascoignes voyage into Holland," which relates
his experiences with shipwreck and with faithless allies, contains several passages of highly realistic poetry. There is no
decoration in his observations of the frightened, seasick soldiers
crossing the channel:

> When I poore soule, whiche close in caban laye,
> And there had reacht till gaule was welneare burste,
> With giddie head, my stumbling steppes must stay
> To looke abroade as boldly as I durste. . . .
> At last the keele which might endure no more,
> Gan rende in twayne and suckt the water in:
> Then might you see pale lookes and wofull cheare,
> Then might you heare loude cryes and deadly dinne: . . .
> (Prouty, 188, 190)

Nor is there any decoration in his description of the reception
given his party by the city: "Wel, at the *Bryell* to tell you what
we fynde,/ The Governour was all bedewed with drinke,/ His
trulls and he were all layde downe to sleepe" (Prouty, 193).
His singular lack of success in the journey is reported in an
apparently straight-forward manner; but considerable irony,
even disgust, can be felt under the narrative:

> They sent us succor saust with sowre despyte,
> They saved our lives and spoylde us of the rest,
> They stale our goods by day and eke by night,
> They shewed the worst and closely kept the best.
> (Prouty, 192)

A third poem exhibiting certain characteristics of his diction,
"Dulce Bellum Inexpertis," discusses warfare with a mixture of

narrative and didacticism. He begins the long poem by telling various groups of people that they would stay out of war if they were wiser and by calling war "the scourge of God." The poem achieves irony throughout much of its content, as he reiterates his title in such lines as "How sweet warre is to such as knowe it not" and "But such as once have fealt the skortching fire,/ Will seldome efte to play with flame desire." And, although modern critics consider Gascoigne to be cold and humorless, we find humor throughout nearly the whole poem. The ridicule of certain attitudes toward war underlies much of the poem and provides some humor just by ironic contrast; but also we find overt humor in the rough, plain description of men in battle as in the following:

> Herewith we had nor powder packt in store,
> Nor flesh, nor fishe, in poudring tubbes yput,
> Nor meale, nor malt, nor meane (what would you more?)
> To get such geare if once we should be shut.
> And God he knowes, the English souldiours gut,
> Must have his fill of victualles once a day,
> Or els he will but homely earne his pay.
>
> (Cunliffe, I, 171)

The language is perhaps crude and is not in the courtly tradition, but the desire to laugh at something coarsely foolish is strong in this stanza, and it appears often. The language employed in all three of the poems is blunt, vivid, and vernacular. There is little refinement to it in the sense that it reflects the influence of Classical or foreign vocabularies. This language is the one used in the world of active men, purified only to the omission of cant phrases and most oaths and devoted to accuracy of description.

Each of these poems discusses warfare and, to a certain extent, the life of a soldier. In his masque, Gascoigne concentrates primarily on the colorful panorama and drama of warfare. To avoid offending the members of the wedding party for whom the masque was written, Gascoigne has the youth view the series of battles and the captures as an exciting adventure, set off by such lines as "The drumes crie dub a dub, the braying trumpets blow." In this way, Gascoigne can work in such brutal details as slicing off the Turk commander's head and raising it aloft on a pike by simply having the boy view it as part of the gory splendor of war. The boy is by no means callous; he is strongly affected by what he sees. But what he sees is strength, honor, gallantry, and the supreme thrill of being a conqueror. When the boy's father dies in battle, the boy is not so much sad as impressed by the courage and honor in fighting to the death against overpowering odds:

> This said, beholde, the Turkes enclosde us round about,
> And seemed to wonder that we durst resist so great a rout. . . .
> And he him selfe which sawe, he might no more abide,
> Did thrust amid the thickest throng, and so with honoure died.
>
> (Prouty, 175)

There is no cynicism at all; warfare is colorful, noble, and idealized. It is a concept which might easily be held by a romantic, courtly knight.

The second poem, "Gascoignes voyage into Hollande," is quite different in tone; for the poet writes from an experienced point of view—the soldier who has returned from an unsuccessful mission. The tone is cynical with some bitterness apparent at times. In the poem, Gascoigne and a troop of English soldiers are robbed, cheated, betrayed, and left to drown by the Dutch. The people they are to fight for are unfriendly, drunken, and completely untrustworthy:

> To tell my Lord this tale now tane in hand,
> As how they traine their treasons all in drinke,
> And when themselves for dronk can scarcely stand,
> Yet sucke out secretes (as themselves do thinke)
> From guests, the best (almost) in all their lande, . . .
> Dissemble deepe, and mocke sometimes the more.
> Well, drunkenesse is here good companye,
> And therewithall *per consequence* it falles,
> That whoredome is accoumpted Jollytie:
> A gentle state, where two such Tenisballes
> Are tossed still and better boules let lye.
>
> (Prouty, 193-94)

In this poem, the only ideals expressed are courage and faithfulness, but generally their absence is what is pointed out. In contrasting the Dutch with the English, only among the English is courage found: "Some englishe were, whose naked swordes did force/ The drunken dutch, the cankred churles to come, . . ./ (Prouty, 192). The poem deals primarily with the faithlessness and treachery of allies, and Gascoigne heaps abuse upon them. In this adventure, Gascoigne has learned much:

> Now ply thee pen, and paint the foule despite
> Of drunken Dutchmen standing there even still,
> For whome we came in their cause for to fight,
> For whom we came their state for to defende,
> For whom we came as friends to grieve their foes,
> They now disdaynd (in this distresse) to lend
> One helping boate for to asswage our woes, ...
> (Prouty, 192)

The longest of the three, "Dulce Bellum Inexpertis," is a less passionate statement of a soldier's problems, but the same themes as in "Gascoignes voyage into Hollande" are present. Here, though, Gascoigne treats them ironically, at times humorously. He seldom lets his tone become bitter. Since this long poem begins with the stated purpose of defining war, he first looks into what other groups of people consider it to be, and then he gives his definition:

> Then what is warre? define it right at last,
> And let us set all olde sayde sawes aside;
> Let Poets lie, let Painters faigne as fast,
> Astronomers let marke how starres do glide,
> And let these Travellers tell wonders wide:
> But let us tell by trustie proufe of truth,
> What thing is warre, which raiseth all this ruth.
>
> And for my parte my fansie for to wright,
> I say that warre is even the scourge of God,
> Tormenting such as dwell in princelie plight,
> Yet not regarde the reaching of his rodde,
> Whose deedes and dueties often times are odde,
> Who raunge at randon, jesting at the just,
> As though they raignde to do even what they lust;
>
> Whome neyther plague can pull into remorse,
> Nor dearth can drawe to mende that is amisse,
> Within whose hearts no pitie findest force,
> Nor right can rule to judge what reason is;
> Whome sicknesse salveth not, nor bale brings blisse:
> Yet can high *Iove* by waste of bloudie warre
> Sende scholemaisters to teach them what they are.
> (Cunliffe, I, 143)

Gascoigne takes the medieval position that war is God's way of punishing a corrupted country. He goes on from this point to warn all the levels of society to beware of the particular corruption that may beset one in their position: the Prince's desire to increase his country's boundaries, and the Duke's desire to own his neighbor's estate. To Gascoigne, the basic cause of war is greed, the desire to increase material wealth; and for greed men are willing to bring down upon themselves and their families the horrors of war because they do not know what war is.

Descending from the cause of war to the types of men anxious to go to war, Gascoigne finds three: haughty hearts, greedy minds, and misers. He looks to history for examples of each and then shows how each type brings about his own doom. An interesting sidelight is the example Gascoigne makes of himself when enumerating the lesser types of men who are forced into soldiering. The ironic humor is apparent in these lines:

> So of the seconde somwhat could I say,
> Howe tattling tungs and busie byting pennes
> Have fledde from Court long sithens many a day,
> And bene full gladde to lurke in *Misers* dennes,
> Some for their owne speech, some for other mennes,
> Some for their books bicause they wrote too much,
> Yea some for rymes, but sure I knowe none such.
>   (Cunliffe, I, 157)

These lines show also that Gascoigne is discussing general types in the first part of the poem rather than making specific and variable observations. He is attempting to show general truths, and for that reason the first half of the poem is highly moral, in many ways satiric, as distinct from the second half, which tells of his experiences directly.

We are more concerned with the second half, for in it Gascoigne tells us what soldiering is actually like. On the purely physical level, the most important elements in a soldier's life are supplies and reinforcements. Gascoigne refers to food and shot often, in the lines quoted above in which the English soldiers must be well fed before they will fight well, and in other lines:

> We had no store of pouder nor of pence,
> Nor meate to eate, nor meane to make defence.

> Here some may say that we were much to bleme, . . .
> And not foresee (how ever went the game)
> Of meate and shotte our souldiours to provide:

And that, before our foes could come so neare,
He would both send us men and merrie cheare.

But, when it came unto the very pinche,
Leyden, farewell! we might for Leyden sterve! ...

They neither gave us meate to feede upon,
Nor drinke, nor powder, pickax, toole nor spade:
So might we sterve, like misers woe-begone,
And fend our foes with blowes of English blade.
For shotte was shronke, and shift could none be made: ...
(Cunliffe, I, 170, 173)

In the realm of values, Gascoigne has learned several basic truths. One, which is consistent with his rather pessimistic philosophy of life, is that "hope" is a misleading, often dangerous state of mind:

Soldiours behold and Captaynes, marke it well,
How hope is harbenger of all mishappe,
Some hope in honour for to beare the bell.
Some hope for gaine and venture many a clappe,
Some hope for trust and light in treasons lappe.
Hope leades the way our lodging to prepare,
Where high mishap (ofte) keepes an Inne of care.
(Cunliffe, I, 169)

A value that Gascoigne does not tell us much about is courage, except to point out to presumed scoffers that he took part in a number of battles: "Yet have I shot at maister *Bellums* butte,/ And throwen his ball, although I toucht no tutte" (Cunliffe I, 159). Of much greater importance to him as a soldier are fidelity and honor. The cause for most of his misfortunes is betrayal by his allies and, to a certain extent, by his men. The betrayal by the Dutch at Leyden, for example, nearly cost him his life and did cause his capture and subsequent return to England without any pay for his years of soldiering. The lack of faith from his allies was reflected in his own men who slandered him upon their return to England:

Straunge tale to tell, we that had set them free,
And set ourselves on sandes for their expence,
We that remaynd in daunger of the tree,
When they were safe—we that were their defence,
With armes, with cost, with deedes, with eloquence:

> We that saved such as knew not where to flie,
> Were now by them accusde of trecherie.
>
> (Cunliffe, I, 188)

Gascoigne was so impressed by the absolute necessity for honor in a man that he was driven to praise even his enemy because he kept his word:

> And by the way, let never *Loques* appeach
> My rayling penne, for thoughe my minde abhorrth
> All Spainish prankes: yet must I thunder forth
> His worthy prayse, who held his fayth unstayned,
> And evermore to us a freend remayned.
>
> (Cunliffe, I, 176)

His final statement of the value of honor appears near the end of the poem, after his experiences have taught him the tenuousness and shallowness of other values. The cruellest wrong that war can do to an individual is to bring his honor under suspicion:

> So losse of goodes shall never trouble me,
> Since God which gives can take when pleaseth him,
> But losse of fame, or slaundred so to be,
> That makes my wittes tobreake above their brimme,
> And frettes my harte, and lames me every limme:
> *For Noble minds their honour more esteeme,*
> *Than worldly wights or wealth or life can deeme.*
>
> Yet in warres such graffes of grudge do grow,
> Such lewdnesse lurkes, such malice makes mischief,
> Such envie boyles, such falshood fire doth blowe,
> That *Bountie* burnes, and truth is called thief,
> And good desertes are brought into such grief,
> That Saunder snuffe which sweares the matter out,
> Brings oftentimes the noblest names in doubt.
>
> (Cunliffe, I, 179)

The basic theme of the poem is to describe the reality of a soldier's life to those who do not know it. It covers the misunderstandings between civilians and soldiers; it discusses the jealousies and greed of the people involved; it tells of Gascoigne's personal frustrations in his attempts to become wealthy; it gives vivid, literal descriptions of battles in progress; and it moralizes generally about the life of a soldier. This poem is the most complete of the three; yet all of them attempt to show the various aspects of warfare and the realities of the soldier's life, from his first romantic imaginings to his trials, hardships, triumphs, and loves—in general, what the world is to a soldier, and what a soldier is to the world. Gascoigne's diction is of importance to his purpose because he establishes through it the tone for each aspect given in the poem. The diction is concrete and pointed with little or no decoration. Because he uses the vernacular language, with its resulting realism, he can brag, curse, and insult; it allows him to describe such things as nausea, drunkenness, and treachery in realistic detail. But most importantly, particularly in the last two poems discussed, his diction allows us to recognize a consistent personality, one strongly flavored with irony and pessimism, yet one resilient enough to find some humor in all the evils of warfare and even retain a certain philosophic bent of mind which allowed him to compose *The Grief of Joye* during the actual fighting.

These poems, taken together, give us a vivid perspective of a whole way of life. Individually, each achieves certain successes, particularly "Dulce Bellum Inexpertis"; but, as we look at all of them, we are able to recognize a pattern to his work, a complete panorama that puts his age in an accurate historical perspective. Thus, his work, taken as a whole, becomes more valuable because, by its very honesty, completeness, and use of realistic detail, we can appreciate more fully the lives of other men with similar backgrounds—such men as Barnaby Rich, Walter Ralegh, and Philip Sidney. In effect, Gascoigne is the poetic spokesman for this type of life in the sixteenth century. In many ways he is the real-life parallel to Falstaff in that he presents the human realities of soldiering—its frustrations, its unpleasantnesses, its petty intrigues, its too frequent rejection of ideals, and its greed. Yet, being real, he was at the same time more complex, so that we see an immature, often wild youth experiencing treachery, love affairs, cowardice, defamation of character, disloyal allies, and capture, yet remaining himself loyal to his superiors and trying to maintain the chivalric ideal of knighthood throughout the whole disillusioning period. The remarkable aspect, one also true of most of his contemporaries, is that he was able to write during this period after all that he had experienced. And, at the end, although he was certainly cynical, he was far from being disillusioned, for he even reiterated those values which he found still held strength.

CHAPTER 6

Gascoigne's Satire: The Steele Glas

IN contrast to what appears on the surface of the literature, the spirit of satire ebbed low in the sixteenth century; and several reasons can be given for it. First, there was no native satiric tradition which writers could fall back on, except for the indistinct influence of Chaucer and Langland. Of course, several poets wrote occasional satire, such as John Skelton and Wyatt; but they in no way established a genre. Second, satiric literature is usually written during times of social and political stability when writers must jolt a contented audience into an awareness of existing evil or immorality. But sixteenth-century England, with its religious controversies, its incipient war with Spain, its revolutionary plots, and its changing social structure, was far from having even the appearance of stability. Playwrights, poets, and pamphleteers were too concerned with discovering the proper spheres for the changing social classes to do much more than attack individuals whose ideas differed from their own.

How, then, can we account for the amount of satiric writing in the century? Does it not contradict the point of the preceding statements? The solution, of course, is that most of the satire appearing in the century is copied from the Latin and Italian satirists, or at least modeled after them. The satire of Ariosto, Plautus, Terence, Juvenal, Persius, Horace, and others was widely admired; and it quickly received English clothes by writers who hoped to gain recognition and positions at court from it. The satire that found its way into the School and Inns of Court plays was quite general and conventional— the ridicule of old men trying to be lovers, of bragging soldiers, of country louts and city parasites, and so forth. The achievement of such plays, as in Shakespeare's *Love's Labour's Lost,* is that the writers often could make the satire reflect English life and thus genuinely engraft the Classical form onto the contemporary problems. When the satire failed to hit home, the production still was highly entertaining. The satiric poets, modeling themselves

96

after Juvenal and Persius, wrote either general complaints or harsh, broad-ranging invective. Their material, of course, was drawn from contemporary English life, but, as in Raleigh's "The Lie," its objects are conventional ones such as the church, the court, lawyers, and physicians.

As the mid-century poets and playwrights continued to diffuse the Classical satire throughout their literature, the satiric attitude became popular by the end of the century so that, under the pens of Nashe, Gabriel Harvey, Bishop Hall, Jonson, Donne, John Marston, and others, English satire came into its own as a method of expressing dissatisfaction with institutions or of attacking specific evils or people. What satire owes to Chaucer and Langland has been pointed out often; but its debt to the sixteenth-century translators, adapters, and experimenters is much more immediate and much more difficut to define.

The importance of Gascoigne's *The Steele Glas* to literary history was recognized as early as 1780 by Wharton when he described it as both blank-verse satire and as a valuable picture of contemporary English life.[1] From that point on, its merit as a social document and as an innovation in the field of English poetry has been focused upon and pointed out, finally and most completely by Cunliffe in the *Cambridge History of English Literature* in which he enumerates all its important historical characteristics, such as its being the first "regular" or "formal" satire in English and the first using blank verse.[2] However, these qualities are extrinsic, and very few readers of sixteenth-century verse or of the whole genre of satire explore the poem for intrinsic poetic merit. Generally, the condemnation of *The Steele Glas* has been harsh and superficial.

Although the errors which various critics of the poem have made will be noted as we progress, one typical example of the type of criticism often made appears in Hugh Walker's *English Satire and Satirists*: "It is among the perversities of literary fame that his *Steele Glas* is known, at least by name, to thousands who have never heard that Wyatt wrote satires."[3] In this instance, the author has assumed a lack of poetic merit without giving sufficient evidence of it, and the resulting ridicule is destructive because it suggests an unfavorable comparison when there may not in fact be a comparison at all. Walker would have been more accurate if he had simply pointed out that, whereas Wyatt's poetry is undobutedly better, his satire is aimed in a different direction, not one vital to the times, and, thereby, unfortunately forgotten by many.

I *The Biographical Base*

A major reason that critics judge *The Steele Glas* unfavorably is that they do not recognize the purpose of the references to the story of Philomene (or Philomela) which begin the poem. The poem begins with an invocation to Philomene: "*O Phylomene,* then helpe me now to chaunt": she is the nighingale of mythology, a bird that conceals itself at night in thickets and whose long and varied song is plaintive and woeful rather than sweet and melodious. The image of the bird is maintained vividly for several hundred lines and then indirectly throughout the poem. Gascoigne uses the Philomela myth as an allegory of his own life and as a means to air his personal complaints. As a result of the publication of *A Hundreth Sundrie Flowres,* which included the scandalous version of *The Adventures of Master F. J.,* Gascoigne's poetry was confiscated, and he was forced to leave the country to avoid being jailed. He was in debt, discredited at court, and involved in legal entanglements concerning his inheritance which he lost, his right to his wife's wealth, and his right to serve in Parliament. Gascoigne's enemies far outnumbered his friends by 1576, and he was unable to find an audience for his verse, or even to gain preferment for it. As he came to view it, both his riotous youth, (which caused his disinheritance and loss of reputation) and the libelous nature of the *Flowres* had so blackened his name that no amount of moralistic writing, letters to "The reverend Divines," or evidence of having reformed his character could again give him the right to publish his verse freely or to reap rewards from it. Thus, Gascoigne finds a number of correlations between his life and the story of Philomene, and he rehearses them symbolically in the opening section of the poem. The marginal notes are mine:

And yet, even as the mighty gods did daine,
For *Philomele,* that thoughe hir tong were cutte,
Yet should she sing a pleasant note sometimes: (restrictions
So have they deignd, by their devine decrees,   against his
That with the stumps of my reproved tong,   poetry)
I may sometimes, *Reprovers* deedes reprove,
And sing a verse, to make them see themselves.

Then thus I sing, this selly song by night,	(loss of
Like *Phylomene,* since that the shining Sunne	royal
Is now eclypst, which wont to lend me light.	favor)

And thus I sing, in corner closely cowcht	(his "libeled"
Like Philomene, since that the stately cowrts,	foes were
Are now no place, for such poore byrds as I.	at court)

And thus I sing, with pricke against my brest,	(a disease,
Like *Philomene,* since that the privy worme,	or perhaps
Which makes me see my reckles youth mispent,	his bad
May well suffise, to keepe me waking still.	conscience)

And thus I sing, when pleasant spring begins,	(critics and
Like *Philomene,* since every janglyng byrd,	detractors)
Which squeaketh loude, shall never triumph so,	
As though my muze were mute and durst not sing.	

And thus I sing, with harmelesse true intent,	(loss of his
Like *Philomene,* when as percase (meane while)	patrimony
The cuckowe suckes mine eggs by foule deceit,	and his
And lickes the sweet, which might have fed	wife's wealth)
me first.	

(Cunliffe, II, 146-47)

Those men who persecuted Gascoigne and chased him long
after he had changed his way of life are likened to Tereus:

> Synce that the line, of that false caytife king,
> (Which ravished fayre *Phylomene* for lust,
> And then cut out, hir trustie tong for hate)
> Lives yet (my Lord) which words I weepe to write.
> They live, they live, (alas the worse my lucke)
> Whose greedy lust, unbridled from their brest,
> Hath raunged long about the world so wyde,
> To finde a pray for their wide open mouthes,
> And me they found, (O wofull tale to tell)
> Whose harmelesse hart, perceivde not their deceit.
> (Cunliffe, II, 144)

The parallel between the story of Philomela and his own
life was obvious to Gascoigne, and he used it as the opening
dramatic frame for the satire. It is this crouching, concealed,
nightingalelike aspect of Gascoigne that recites the remainder
of the poem: "And thus I meane, in mournfull wise to sing, . . ./
A playne song note, which cannot warble well" (Cunliffe, II,

147). However, after these lines the nightingale image softens, and the poet is distinctly Gascoigne. Why he goes to such lengths to establish the parallel is puzzling, for it serves no function for the bulk of the poem; but it does satisfy his need to display his personal complaint.

The opening device has another interesting aspect in that it allows him to discuss the nature of satire. "Satyra," he says is the twin of "Poesy," and had for parents "Playne dealying" and "Simplycitie," which he explains in a note: "Not ignorant symplicity, but a thought free from deceite." Gascoigne points out that Satyra's speech was plain and of "trustie truth," whereas Poesy's was pleasant and surpassed Satyra's to the extent that "vayne Delight" addressed his suit to Poesy. Poesy, of course, is lyric poetry. Vayne Delight marries Poesy and they settle down at court; but he soon tires of her and seeks another diversion, which happens to be Satyra. However, Satyra is ruined by his attention, is slandered and made suspect, so that her tongue is cut out and she is banished from the court. Gascoigne considers satire to be a form of poetry, but less attractive and pleasant than lyric poetry; and, in the hands of irresponsible people, satire can be malicious and cruel. Satire is supposed to show truth in a plain and simple way, speaking directly and without any subterfuge or decoration.

Gascoigne makes several comments about the function of satire, and he has no illusions about its effectiveness. In the more closely autobiographical section, he mentions that he is to "reprove" men's deeds and words. That is, satire is supposed to scold men for wrongdoing. But this statement is only a part of his concept of satire. How is the satirist to do this? The answer is to hold up a mirror so that men can see themselves as they really are; the satirist is to distinguish both the show and the reality, both what man seems to be and what he really is. This idea establishes another problem, for when the satirist has shown, for example, that the apparently pious churchman is actually seeking material goods, he must have a standard by which to reprove or chastise him; the fact of hypocrisy is not enough. Thus, one of the major criticisms of Gascoigne—that he is old-fashioned, that he did not understand his changing times—arises; for he seems to return to the standards of a feudal-istic, paternal social philosophy, one which utilizes the four estates and upholds the old class structure. He indicates this predilection in the following lines:

> Againe I see, within my glasse of Steele,
> But foure estates, to serve eche country Soyle,
> The King, the Knight, the Pesant, & the Priest
> The King should care for al the subjectes still,
> The Knight should fight, for to defende the same,
> The Peasant he, should labor for their ease,
> And Priests shuld pray, for them & for themselves.
>   (Cunliffe, II, 150)

Kernan, in *The Cankered Muse,* points out that it is characteristic of satirists to look back in history to a stabler time for their social values: "What he calls 'progress' is of no interest to him, for he is always a conservative who calls not for experimentation and social change but for a return to the time-tested virtues . . . which have been perverted or abandoned by greedy man."[4]

Gascoigne certainly looked back to history for many of his values, but this purpose is too simple to explain his object in *The Steele Glas.* For example, although Prouty says that "Gascoigne looked back to the days when the world was well ordered, when the eldest son of a knight would have fared better,"[5] and although Gascoigne himself suggests such an attitude in speaking of rough sailors—"That manners make, them give their betters place./ And use good words, though deeds be nothing gay," (Cunliffe, II, 170)—yet he contradicts the concept of a rigid class structure in the lines: "The greater Birth, the greater glory sure,/ If deeds mainteine, their auncestors degree" (Cunliffe, II, 167). The point is that Gascoigne does not simply advocate a return to an earlier period; the two lines above rule that out. Instead, what guides him is a system of values grounded in honesty, humility, individual rather than inherited worth, and magnanimity of mind. Thus, his first step in the satire is to show the ills of various levels of society; his second step is to show the ideal states of society based on these values.

Before we discuss the main body of *The Steele Glas,* however, we should emphasize the fact that the poem arises from Gascoigne's personal feelings and experiences; it is not simply "a kind of moral poem,"[6] an exercise done merely to gain or regain preferment, as many of his detractors have believed. His self-awareness appears often; shortly after the highly autobiographical Philomene section, he devotes twenty lines to a bluntly realistic self-description with two side notes pointing out their purpose, the first telling whom the lines are about and the second giving the reason for them: "The aucthor himself"; and, "He which will rebuke other mens faults, shal do well not to/ forget hys owne imperfections" (Cunliffe, II, 148).

Again, in a direct reference to his inability to get forgiveness for the errors he made in his youth, Gascoigne tells the priests to pray for the nobility, counsellors, and magistrates, all of whom had helped ruin him:

> Pray, pray, (my priests) that neither love nor mede
> Do sway their minds, from furdering of right,
> That they be not, too saintish nor too sowre,
> But beare the bridle, evenly betwene both,
> That stil they stoppe, one eare to heare him speake,
> Which is accused, absent as he is:
> That evermore, they mark what moode doth move
> The mouth which makes, the information,
> That faults forpaste (so that they be not huge,
> Nor do exceed, the bonds of loyaltie)
> Do never quench their charitable minde,
> When as they see, repentance hold the reines,
> Of heady youth, which wont to runne astray.
>   (Cunliffe, II, 167)

In these lines specific complaints are aired, such as his being tried in England for slander while at the wars in Holland. Yet, the tone is not petulant nor aggrieved; it is objective to the point that a reader without biographical information would miss the allusions completely. Gascoigne used material from his own experience to give the poem's details an impression of reality. He does not show how he has been reformed, nor does he preach a moral; he adapts the details of a specific wrong to point out the general corruption of an aspect of society.

II The "Glass" Frame

Little comment has been made by critics about Gascoigne's use of the device of the glass except to point out its lack of originality and to name some other sources of it; for there is nothing unusual in using a glass, or mirror, as a means to present a pointed story from history. However, as Miss Campbell points out in the introduction to her edition of *The Mirror for Magistrates*, the function of the mirror device is to teach through the presentation

of well-developed historical examples. Gascoigne uses quite a few
historical examples, but he merely cites them; he does not develop
their details to any length. What is more, Miss Campbell says:
"And it must be borne in mind that the usefulness of the
Mirror as a vehicle for political doctrine depended upon the
assumption that God's justice was eternally the same, so that
history did repeat itself in discernible patterns of sin and divine
vengeance for sin."[7]

Gascoigne's use of the mirror, or glass, is rather to point out in
a short space a variety of human and social flaws; he has no
interest in political satire, other than the most general of types;
and the only retribution he suggests for sins is that which might
follow any general weakening of a society's moral fiber. The
point is that Gascoigne's mirror is not quite like the earlier ones.
His is more versatile, and it allows him to organize the poem in a
useful and interesting way. Kernan's statement about *The Steele
Glas*—"But the medieval framework, the 'mirror,' is still employed, . . ."[8] is not correct in the sense that the device is used
solely to reflect historical situations for didactic purposes. Gascoigne uses the device in a more modern way.

The interesting addition that Gascoigne makes, one which
critics pay little attention to, is to use two glasses or mirrors:
the steel glass and the crystal one. Prouty mentions it, but only
to point out, misleadingly, that Gascoigne drops the device soon
after he introduces it.[9] Yet, it is just this dual use upon which
much of the poem is organized; for, as symbols, the two different
glasses stand for the two poles of perception: the appearance,
either actual or wished for; and the reality beneath the appearance, either actual or ideal. Although the crystal glass is not
mentioned in the latter part of the poem, the idea of it is established early; and, whenever the poet tells us he is peering into
his steel glass, we are prepared to accept it as the glass of truth
as contrasted to the glass of foolish pride and hypocrisy. Gascoigne does not need to mention the crystal glass often, for the
contrast to truth which it symbolizes remains apparent throughout the poem.

The device of the two different glasses is established shortly
after the Philomene section, and it is developed in various points
in the poem. He establishes it in this way:

> I see and sigh, (bycause it makes me sadde)
> That pevishe pryde, doth al the world possesse,

> And every wight, will have a looking glasse
> To see himselfe, yet so he seeth him not: ...
> That age is deade, and vanisht long ago,
> Which thought that steele, both trusty was & true,
> And needed not, a foyle of contraries,
> But shewde al things, even as they were in deede.
> In steade whereof, our curious yeares can finde
> The christal glas, which glimseth brave & bright,
> Beguylde with foyles, of sundry subtil sights,
> So that they seeme, and covet not to be.
> (Cunliffe, II, 147-48)

These lines show the essential contrast between the two ways
of looking at the world: the foolish, optimistic, conceited way;
and the realistic way. The result is that, because people think or
wish themselves to be more than they are, society and individuals
decay:

> This is the cause (beleve me now my Lorde)
> That Realmes do rewe, from high prosperity,
> That kings decline, from princely government,
> That Lords do lacke, their auncestors good will,
> That knights consume, their patrimonie still, ...
> (Cunliffe, II, 148)

He develops the concept of the steel glass further to heighten
another important contrast:

> [Lucylius] gan bequeath, a glass of trustie Steele,
> Wherin they may be bolde alwayes to looke,
> Bycause it shewes, all things in their degree.
> And since myselfe (now pride of youth is past)
> Do love to be, and let al seeming passe,
> Since I desire, to see my selfe indeed,
> Not what I would, but what I am or should,
> Therefore I like this trustie glasse of Steele.
> (Cunliffe, II, 149)

Here we see that the steel glass tells us not only what we are,
but also what we should be, as contrasted to the crystal glass
which shows us what we wish to be. The steel glass, then, has a
moral function: it shows us the morally ideal world as well as
the actual world so that we can change our ways to achieve it.
The crystal glass is doubly dangerous in that it shows us both
what we think we are and what we would like to be apart from
any moral restrictions; yet, it hides the dangers implicit in such

an irresponsible attitude. He emphasizes this point in a passage
on kings:

> And christal glosse, doth glister so therewith,
> That Kings conceive, their care is wonderous great
> When as they beat, their busie restles braynes,
> To maintaine pompe, and high triumphant sights,
> To fede their fil, of daintie delicates, . . .
> To delve the ground, for mines of glistering golde:
> And never care, to maynteine peace and rest,
> To yeld reliefe, where needy lacke appears,
> To stop one eare until the poore man speake,
> To seeme to sleepe, when Justice still doth wake,
> To gard their lands, from sodaine sword and fier, . . .
>
> (Cunliffe, II, 150-51)

In this passage, pride, vanity, and foolish optimism conspire to
prevent the king from seeing his duty and from carrying it out.
The crystal glass shows only the temporal, immediate, pleasur-
able things of life, as Gascoigne says further on: "O Christal
Glasse, thou settest things to shew, / Which are (God knoweth)
of little worth in dede" (Cunliffe, II, 153). Finally, in the last
reference to the crystal glass, he reiterates the basic difference
between the two glasses:

> The country Squire, doth covet to be Knight,
> The Knight a Lord, the Lord an Erle or a Duke,
> The Duke a King, the King would Monarke be,
> And none content, with that which is his own.
> Yet none of these, can see in Christal glasse
> (Which glistereth bright, & Bleares their gasing eyes)
> How every life, beares with him his disease,
> But in my glasse, which is of trustie steele,
> I can perceive, how kingdomes breede but care,
> How Lordship lives, with lots of lesse delight, . . .
> Than common people finde in every coast.
>
> (Cunliffe, II, 153-54)

The steel glass enables us to look through superficial appear-
ances and see the underlying realities.

Once Gascoigne has established the contrast between the two
glasses, he implies the contrast each time he refers to his steel
glass. Thus, we are constantly aware of the appearance-reality
theme as we read through the poem, and this awareness allows
him to use the glass in several different ways. For example, in

his steel glass he sees what soldiers ought to be, and in this way
he can criticize what they actually are:

> But if you wil, constraine me for to speake,
> What souldiours are, or what they ought to be
> (And I my selfe, of that profession)
> I see a crew, which glister in my glasse,
> The bravest bande, that ever yet was sene: . . .
> I see not one therin, which seekes to heape
> A world of pence, by pinching of dead payes, . . .
> I see not one, within this glasse of mine,
> Whose fethers flaunt, and flicker in the winde,
> As though he were, all onely to be markt, . . .
>   (Cunliffe, II, 155-56)

Also, he can look into his steel glass to find examples from history,
either good or bad, to substantiate the particular value he is
discussing. Using the passage in which he criticizes bad soldiers
again, he shows examples of good ones: "Behold behold, where
Pompey commes before, / Where *Manlius,* and *Marius* insue, /
AEmilius and *Curius* I see, . . ." (Cunliffe, II, 155). In the same
passage, he gives examples of the evils which befall bad soldiers:

> O Captayns come, and Souldiours come apace
> Behold my glasse, and you shall see therin,
> Proud *Crassus* bagges, consumde by covetise,
> Greate Alexander, drounde in drunkennesse,
> *Caesar* and *Pompey,* spilt with privy grudge,
> *Brennus* beguild, with lightnesse of beliefe,
> *Cleomenes,* by ryot not regarded, . . .
>   (Cunliffe, II, 158)

This technique is similar to the standard device of using a mirror
to teach by showing examples from history, as done in *A Mirror
for Magistrates.* However, Gascoigne simplifies the technique; he
merely mentions a person's name and a familiar detail about that
person, without reviewing a whole history.

The glass also is used to criticize by default. He recounts
the many good characteristics of merchants under Emperor
August IX, such as lending their goods at a reasonable rate; and,
when he says "These knackes (my lord) I cannot cal to minde, /
Bycause they shewe not in my glasse of steel" (Cunliffe, II, 163),
he accuses contemporary merchants of the opposite characteristics, of the abuses which he says the Roman merchants did not

practice. His failure to see favorable characteristics in his glass of truth becomes, therefore, an indictment.

The last way he uses the glass is simply to look into it to see truthful descriptions of various classes of people. He describes officers, lawyers, merchants, and priests as he sees them parade across his view: "But holla: here, I see a wondrous sight, / I see a swarme of Saints within my glasses" (Cunliffe, I, 164). This final use of the glass is also the simplest. By seeing these groups in the glass of truth, he is able to spot their flaws, conceits, ridiculous aspects, hypocrisies, and deceits. Thus, to the extent that he relies on the device of the glass in these sections, his satire rests on whatever he can include in a simple description.

It is true that Gascoigne shifts his handling of the glass device somewhat as the poem progresses. In those passages in which he uses the two mirrors—the crystal and the steel—he is able to produce greater irony and tension; the satire, or implied criticism, rests more on the structure of the poem than on the rhetoric. As the concept of the crystal mirror fades, the satire depends more on the effectiveness of the poet's expression than on any tension produced through implied contradiction. It is unfortunate that close readers of *The Steele Glas* have not given more importance to the crystal one; indeed, many critics tend to disregard it entirely. Thus, they miss the key method Gascoigne uses to organize the poem. If we look at the over-all poem, we find that the dual-mirror device is used when the poet discusses men's minds and analyzes their psychology; the single mirror is used when the poet describes outward things, the results of flaws in men's minds. The last part of the satire lists the faults of society; the first part gives the reason for them. Without an understanding of the crystal glass, we are not aware of the most important, if not the most interesting, part of the poem.

III   *The Satire*

As we can see, then, the over-all organization of the poem is based upon two mirrors; the crystal mirror shows the faults lying within men, and the steel mirror shows the faults in the outside world resulting from these inner flaws. By far the greatest part of the poem is devoted to describing what the poet sees in his steel glass, and we get a very complete picture of the England of Gascoigne's time. However, Gascoigne is not satisfied simply to show the social evils; he attempts to reinforce them by con-

trasting several of the major flaws of his society with their perfect
states. To do so, he is forced to turn to ancient times to find a
golden age, and he discovers a number of Classical examples
which contrast effectively with what he sees in England. After
his criticism of the state of the English court, for example, he says:

> In olden dayes, good kings and worthy dukes,
> (Who sawe themselves, in glasse of trusty Steele)
> Contented were, with pompes of little pryce,
> And set their thoughtes, on regal government.
>
> An order was, when Rome did florish most,
> That no man might triumph in stately wise,
> But such as had, with blowes of bloudy blade
> Five thousand foes in foughten field foredone,
> Now he that likes, to loke in Christal glasse,
> May see proud pomps, in high triumphant wise,
> Where never blowe, was delt with enemie.
>   (Cunliffe, II, 151)

Again, when he points out the greed, thievery, and lust found
among the English soldiers, he points to a contrasting parallel
in ancient history. Thus, covetous soldiers are contrasted to
Paulus Æmilius; cruel soldiers, to Pericles, who rejoiced in clemency; braggarts, to Manlius, who had received thirty wounds
but seldom mentioned them; drunken soldiers, to Augustus
Caesar.

In one sense, Gascoigne's desire to include in his satire all
levels of English life tends to lessen the immediacy of his satire.
His technique is to summarize flaws and then to contrast them
with a social ideal taken from history so that the realization of
these flaws will be heightened. But, in summarizing the flaws, he
falls into the pitfall of oversimplification, at least in the first part
of his satire; and several of his criticisms are misleading or inconsequential. For example, following the lines naming the four
estates, quoted earlier, he rehearses the faults found in bad kings
and princes. He accuses them of being too interested in material
pleasures:

> To maintaine pompe, and high triumphant sights,
> To fede their fil, of dainty delicates,
> To glad their harts, with sight of pleasant sports,
> To fil their eares, with sound of instruments,
> To breake with bit, the hot coragious horse,

> To deck their haules, with sumpteous cloth of gold,
> To cloth themselves, with silkes of straunge devies, . . .
>   (Cunliffe, II, 150-51)

Gascoigne apparently had the activities of the court society in mind, for these criticisms are more appropriately those of the entire court than of Queen Elizabeth. He really had no direct experience with bad kingship, and the failings of historical kings did not prompt any feelings of outrage. The following lines suggest, of course, why he held back from criticizing the English kings:

> I speake not this, by any english king,
> Nor by our Queene, whose high forsight provides,
> That dyre debate, is fledde to foraine Realmes,
> Whiles we injoy the golden fleece of peace.
>   (Cunliffe, II, 151)

His experiences with knights and gentlemen are more immediate, and his criticisms of them are much more direct than are those of kings:

> The Gentleman, which might in countrie keepe
> A plenteous boorde, and feed the fatherlesse,
> With pig and goose, with mutton, beefe and veale, . . .
> Will breake up house, and dwel in market townes,
> A loytring life, and like an *Epicure.* . . .
>
> The stately lord, which woonted was to kepe
> A court at home, is now come up to courte,
> And leaves the country for a common prey,
> To pilling, pulling, brybing, and deceit:
> (Al which his presence might have pacified,
> Or else have made offenders smel the smoke.)
>   (Cunliffe, II, 154)

In these lines, we see a similarity to his other poem with like satiric comment, "Dominus ijs opus habet." The point of the satire in both is the same, that landed noblemen were avoiding their responsibilities, with a consequent disorientation of goals: "But who (meane while) defends the common welth? / Who rules the flocke, when sheperds so are fled? / Who stayes the staff, which shuld uphold the state?" (Cunliffe, II, 154). Gascoigne felt keenly the evil results of the general change in the structure of English society which brought the landowners to the city, but he never understood the causes of the change.

110

Nor was he better able to understand the reasons behind his
own youthful desire to sell part of his inheritance in order to buy
a career at court. A number of poems rehearse this aspect of his
life—such poems as the non-satiric "Complaint of the green
knight" and "Gascoignes wodmanship," and the partly satiric
"Magnum vectigal parcimonia" and *Sat cito, si sat bene*—and
we find it used as a lesson in this same section of *The Steele Glas*:

> And now the youth which might have served him,
> In comely wise, with countrey clothes yclad, . . .
> Is faine to sell, his landes for courtly cloutes,
> Or else sits still, and liveth like a loute,
> (Yet of these two, the last fault is the lesse:)
> And so those imps which might in time have sprong
> Alofte (good lord) and servde to shielde the state,
> Are either nipt, with such untimely frosts,
> Or else growe crookt, bycause they be not proynd.
>   (Cunliffe, II, 154-55)

The parenthetical line emphasizes Gascoigne's own experience.
He sees the error of his choice and the evil results of it; but,
caught in the middle of a current of change, he is aware of neither
its origin nor its destination, only that he is in it.

A reason for the greater realism of the details in this section is
that his range of experience includes them, just as his experience
includes the frivolities of court life, the major object of his attack on kingship. The more abstract, or less immediate, areas
of his satire deal with such vices as covetousness and avarice;
and, because they are the traditional targets of the satirist, they
do not demand details gleaned from direct experience. Gascoigne
handles such satire fairly well, but without the power and urgency
of expression that we find in the passages dealing with his observations of contemporary England and Englishmen. The following lines could be aptly applied to almost any period of
history:

> But glittring gold, which many yeares lay hidde, . . .
> Hath now enflamde, the noblest Princes harts
> With foulest fire, of filthy Avarice,
> And seldome seene, that kings can be content
> To kepe their bounds, which their forefathers left:
> What causeth this, but greedy golde to get?
> Even gold, which is, the very cause of warres,
> The neast of strife, and nourice of debate,

> The barre of heaven, and open way to hel.
> But is this strange? when Lords when Knights & Squires . . .
> Are not afrayd to covet like a King?
>
> (Cunliffe, II, 153)

These lines, although showing power and a firm grasp of the subject, are general, not particular, and could easily be found in the satire of several historical periods.

When Gascoigne turns to the use of Classical examples, as he does throughout the first two-thirds of the poem, we receive the impression that his purpose is less to satirize than to provide moral instruction; and this use gives a curious effect to the poem, for it combines effective scolding with ineffective example. A decrease of effect can be seen in the passage on drunken soldiers, in which Gascoigne, certainly because of his own soldiering experiences, conveys a strong sense of outrage, a sense which is vitiated by the subsequent Classical example. The first part is vivid and realistic; the second part, bookish:

> What should I speake, of drunken Soldiours?
> Or lechers lewde, which fight for filthy lust?
> Of whom that one, can sit and bybbe his fil,
> Consume his coyne, (which might good corage yeld,
> To such as march, and move at his commaunde)
> And makes himselfe, a worthy mocking stocke
> Which might deserve, (by sobre life) great laude.
> That other dotes, and driveth forth his dayes
> In vaine delight, and foule concupiscence,
> When works of weight, might occupie his hedde.
> Yea therwithal, he puts his owne fonde heade
> Under the belt, of such as should him serve,
> And so becoms, example of much evil,
> Which should have servde, as lanterne of good life:
> And is controlde, wheras he should commaund.
> *Augustus Caesar*, he which might have made
> Both feasts and banquets bravely as the best,
> Was yet content (in campe) with homely cates,
> And seldom drank his wine unwatered.
>
> (Cunliffe, II, 157-58)

Gascoigne gives Classical examples to chastise officers, peasants, false judges, advocates, and merchants. But when he comes to the last two, the poem's structure takes a decided turn away from Classical examples to concentrate on naming the faults the poet finds in the surrounding society. Beginning with the section on the advocate, Gascoigne ceases instructing by example and begins criticizing by ironic contrast, the last major technique of the poem. The advocates are contrasted directly to Brutus, Marcus Crassus, Cicero, and Demosthenes; but rather than telling stories of the four, Gascoigne assumes our knowledge of them and begins to build the type of ironic contrast that characterizes the remainder of the poem:

> Where shal we reade, that any of these foure
> Did ever pleade, as carelesse of the trial?
> Or who can say, they builded sumpteously?
> Or wroong the weake, out of his own by wyles? . . .
> They did not rowte (like rude unringed swine,)
> To roote nobilitie from heritage.
> They stoode content, with gaine of glorious fame,
> (Bycause they had, respect to equitie)
> To leade a life, like true Philosophers.
> (Cunliffe, II, 162)

The criticism of contemporary lawyers is most obvious in the lines "They did not rowte (like rude unringed swine,) / To roote nobilitie from heritage." If *The Steele Glas* could be termed only a "moral poem," the justification for it would have to rest on the straightforward use of Classical examples to teach various morals. But at this point in the poem, the epithet loses its meaning; for, as in the above example, Gascoigne attacks a contemporary practice with both irony and invective. From here to the end of the poem, the intent is to attack social evils, not to teach moral precepts; and, to do so, he uses a combination of irony, invective, and ridicule. In his description of his ideal priests, for example, he uses an implied ironic contrast effectively:

> These be my priests, . . .
> Which are not proude, nor covet to be riche.
> Which go not gay, nor fede on daintie foode,
> Which envie not, nor knowe what malice meanes,
> Which loth all lust, disdayning drunkenesse,
> Which cannot faine, which hate hypocrisie.
> (Cunliffe, II, 164)

In his long catalogue of social wrongs, he states the faults directly: "When smithes shoo horses, as they would be shod, / when millers, toll not with a golden thumbe, / when bakers make, not barme beare price of wheat, . . . (Cunliffe, II, 171). Finally, in the epilogue he uses strong invective when he de-

scribes the women of the court, a subject he discusses in several
other poems with equal heat;

> Beholde (my lorde) what monsters muster here,
> With Angels face, and harmefull helish harts,
> With smyling lookes, and depe deceitful thoughts,
> With tender skinnes, and stony cruel mindes,
> With stealing steppes, yet forward feete to fraude.
> Behold, behold, they never stande content,
> With God, with kinde, with any helpe of Arte,
> But curle their locks, with bodkins & with braids,
> But dye their heare, with sundry subtill sleights,
> But paint and slicke, til fayrest face be foule,
> But bumbast, bolster, frisle, and perfume:
> They marre with muske, the balme which nature made,
> And dig for death, in dellicatest dishes.
> (Cunliffe, II, 173)

In these examples, particularly in the last one, Gascoigne's object
is distinctly to satirize rather than to teach. We do not say that
he does not wish to erase the faults which he finds; but his
method is not the straightforward method of the moralist. His
is the oblique method of the satirist who is willing to tear down
institutions, if necessary, so that better ones can be built.

IV *The English Flavor*

Throughout *The Steele Glas*, Gascoigne is aware of his position
as an English poet, and he takes some pains to give the poem a
strong English character. One method he uses is to draw material
from his own experiences. From his observations, Gascoigne
concluded that the basic disease infecting all levels of life was
a mixture of pride, foolish optimism, greed, and hypocrisy; and
his descriptions of the symptoms of this disease in England provide us with a vivid picture of contemporary English life at
nearly all social levels. At court, he found pride and foolish
optimism:

> Our bumbast hose, our treble double ruffes,
> Our sutes of Silke, our comely garded capes,
> Our knit silke stockes, and spanish lether shoes,
> (Yea velvet serves, ofttimes to trample in)
> Our plumes, our spangs, and al our queint aray,
> Are pricking spurres, provoking filthy pride,
> And snares (unseen) which leade a man to hel.
> (Cunliffe, II, 152-53)

Among soldiers, he found pride and greed:

> I see not one therin, which seekes to heape
> A world of pence, by pinching of dead payes,
> And so beguiles, the prince in time of nede,
> When muster day, and foughten fielde are odde. . . .
>
> I see not one, within this glasse of mine,
> Whose fethers flaunt, and flicker in the winde,
> As though he were, all onely to be markt,
> When simple snakes, which go not halfe so gay,
> Can leave him yet a furlong in the field: . . .
>
> (Cunliffe, II, 155-56)

Among merchants, he found greed:

> And master Merchant, he whose travaile ought
> Commodiously, to doe his countrie good,
> And by his toyle, the same for to enriche,
> Can finde the meane, to make *Monopolyes*
> Of every ware, that is accompted strange.
>
> (Cunliffe, II, 162)

At the universities, he found pride:

> Pray for the nources, of our noble Realme,
> I meane the worthy Universities, . . .
> That *Philosophy*, smel no secret smoke,
> Which *Magike* makes, in wicked mysteries:
> That *Logike* leape, not over every stile,
> Before he come, a furlong neare the hedge, . . .
> That *Sophistrie*, do not deceive it selfe, . . .
>
> (Cunliffe, II, 168)

It must be granted that the qualities of pride, greed, and foolish optimism are common to all men; but, in the examples given above, the descriptions are not abstractions: they are real-life details, and they gain in vividness and color because of it. The English flavor is strongest at the end of the poem where he lists methods by which professional men, merchants, and artisans cheat the public. In answer to a priest's question of when they could stop praying for England, Gascoigne answers with a fifty-seven-line passage, in the following manner:

> I tel thee (priest) when shoomakers make shoes,
> That are wel sowed, with never a stitch amisse,
> And use no crafte, in uttring of the same:

> When Taylours steale, no stuffe from gentlemen,
> When Tanners are, with Corriers wel agreede,
> And both so dresse their hydes, that we go dry: . . .
>
> When mercers make, more bones to swere and lye,
> When vintners mix, no water with their wine,
> When printers passe, none errours in their bookes,
> When hatters use, to bye none olde cast robes, . . .
>
> When auditours, their counters cannot change,
> When proude surveyours, take no parting pens,
> When Silver sticks not on the tellers fingers,
> And when receivers, pay as they receive,
> When al these folke, have quite forgotten fraude.
>   (Cunliffe, II, 171-72)

In this listing, we can see the tricks of the political, mercantile, and professional Englishman, tricks which perhaps had been used for centuries. There is no allusion to outside literatures here; the section is entirely English. Fraud and hypocrisy run free, and the entire value system has increase of wealth as its foundation. Gascoigne accepts it while he condemns it; he recognizes the appearance of this materialistic goal and castigates its reality. And, in doing so, he left behind a valuable record of sixteenth-century English life.

Another way *The Steele Glas* achieves its English tone is its attack on the southern countries of Europe, mainly Italy. Gascoigne holds the Englishman's traditional contempt for the supposed immorality of these countries, and he expresses it several times throughout the poem, although the focus of the attack varies. At one point, he accuses the court entertainment of falling under corrupt influence when he decries "these newe Italian sportes." In his direct references to them, he is cool toward Spain, France, and Portugal; but he uses the familiar invective in his comments on Italy. In the following lines, the poet tells the priests to pray for the princes of each country:

> Tell some (in *Spaine*) how close they kepe their closets,
> How selde the winde, doth blow upon their cheeks,
> While as (meane while) their sunburnt sutours sterve
> And pine before, their processe be preferrde. . . .
>
> Tel some (in *France*) how much they love to dance,
> While sutours daunce, attendaunce at the dore. . . .

> Tel some (in *Portugale*) how colde they be,
> In setting forth, of right religion:
> Which more esteme, the present pleasures here,
> Then stablishing, of God his holy worde. . . .

> Tel some (*Italian*) princes, how they winke
> At stinking stews, and say they are (forsooth)
> A remedy, to quench foule filthy luste:
> When as in dede they be the sinkes of sinne.
>   (Cunliffe, II, 167-68)

Gascoigne held, however, very little love for any of the Continental countries. His attitude toward the Dutch is discussed in another chapter, and in "Gascoignes councell given to master Bartholmew Withipol," besides reiterating his attitude toward Italy, he makes several unfavorable comments about Spain:

> Some may presente thee with a pounde or twayne
> Of Spanishe soape to washe thy lynnen white:[10]
> Beware therefore, and thynke it were small gayne,
> To save thy shirte, and caste thy skinne of quite:
> Some cunning man maye teache thee for to ryde,
> And stuffe thy saddle all with Spanishe wooll,
> Or in thy stirrops have a toye so tyde,
> As bothe thy legges may swell thy buskins full: . . .
>   (Prouty, 169)

In these examples, Gascoigne is reiterating a quite common position held by English writers before and after him.

Another way in which *The Steele Glas* gains its English flavor is through its diction. Gascoigne consciously attempts to keep his diction as traditionally English as possible. To do so, he uses archaic words and word forms, and monosyllabic words. He avoids ornate and Italianate diction and uses few foreign words or "inkhornisms." By using occasional phrases with a specific local reference, he creates a certain English tone, as in the following lines:

> He that can share, from every pention payde
> A Peeter peny weying halfe a pound, . . .
> How ere their gownes, be gathred in the backe,
> With organe, pipes, of old king Henries clamp.
>   (Cunliffe, II, 160)

But perhaps the element that most overtly gives the poem its English flavor is Gascoigne's use of Piers Plowman.[11] It must be pointed out here that the name "Piers Plowman" bears greater importance to modern readers than it did to Gascoigne, for he uses it solely to refer to the English farming peasant; he does not use it to recall Langland's satire as many critics have believed. Except for suggesting a common social station, Langland's "Piers" and Gascoigne's "Peerce" are used in entirely different ways. Langland's "Piers" is an individual person who perceives, criticizes, and participates to some extent in dramatic situations; Gascoigne's "Peerce" is the name given to a category of people being discussed. Gascoigne uses the name in the same way he uses other names—David Diker for the common laborer; Hick, Hobbe, and Dick for common country louts. In fact, Gascoigne is unsure whether the plowman or the sailor is more representative of the common Englishman; he chooses the plowman only because no sailor can live without the fruits of the plow, whereas the opposite is not so. As he discusses the plowman, he does not hesitate to list his faults as well as his virtues. There is a slight resemblance to be seen with Langland—for example, Gascoigne uses the example of the plowman to chastise the clergy—but the emphasis is definitely on the English peasant's cheating and fraudulent ways; and the only good aspect of him worthy to be mentioned is the fact that he does provide food for the country. The English flavor is quite strong in the following lines:

> Behold him (priests) & though he stink of sweat
> Disdaine him not: for shal I tel you what?
> Such clime to heaven, before the shaven crownes.
> But how? forsooth, with true humilytie.
> Not that they hoord, their grain when it is cheape,
> Nor that they kill, the calfe to have the milke,
> Nor that they set, debate betwene their lords,
> By earing up the balks, that part their bounds:
> Nor for because, they can both crowche & creep
> (The guilefulst men, that ever God yet made)
> When as they meane, most mischiefe and deceite,
> Nor that they can, crie out on landelordes lowde,
> And say they racke, their rents an ace to high,
> When they themselves, do sel their landlords lambe
> For greater price, then ewe was wont be worth.
> I see you Peerce, my glasse was lately scowrde.
> But for they feed, with fruites of their gret paines,
> Both King and Knight, and priests in cloyster pent:
> Therefore I say, that sooner some of them

> Shal scale the walles which leade us up to heaven,
> Than cornfed beasts, whose bellie is their God,
> Although they preach, of more perfection.
>   (Cunliffe, II, 170)

It is quite important to recognize that Gascoigne intentionally used certain methods in order to give *The Steele Glas* an English character. Unlike Wyatt, Gascoigne does not advocate a retreat to the country in order to avoid the evils of city life; he desires, instead, a smoothly functioning social order, one with an emphasis on a medieval hierarchy, to be sure, but one based on the values of honesty, truth, and justice—virtues he believed to be inherited from the past. He tried to establish an almost patriotic alliance with the past, hoping perhaps to find a source of strength there that he did not find in the present. But it would be unfair to stop at this point, for Gascoigne does not just wish to reverse the trend of history. What he does want to do is to correct the faults and vices that he finds in society, and to do this he must have some standard to rest upon—again, the values that he found only in history, and usually in Classical history at that. To some extent he succeeds, in such places as telling the Cambridge scholars to have more love for their native tongue, and in criticizing the outrageous behavior of courtiers. But his value as a satirist lies chiefly in the broad range of his satire, in the particularity of the details he used. At no one place is Gascoigne's perception unusually keen; breadth of vision rather than depth recommends the poem to us.

CHAPTER 7

The Adventures of Master F. J.

G ASCOIGNE'S *The Adventures of Master F. J.* is certainly one of the period's most interesting works for a variety of reasons. One of England's first novels, it offers several unusual and effective devices in its narrative technique. It satirizes the courtly traditions and Petrarchan poetic conventions in a vital and shrewdly humorous way. Also, it has an unusual bibliographical history which, when untangled, illuminates aspects of both Gascoigne's life and the society within which he was writing. Unfortunately, modern readers have a difficult time finding a copy of *The Adventures*; the available ones utilize the bowdlerized second version which eliminates not only the more interesting symbolic and sexual parts of the original but also much of the humorous and often biting satire, and which adds a moral and somewhat artificial ending to the story. The second version has not found great popularity among modern readers.

I *Bibliographical Problems*

The original *Adventures* appeared in 1573 as part of *A Hundreth Sundrie Flowres*.[1] At first, *The Hundreth Sundrie Flowres* was widely believed to be the work of many hands. The format presents us with an editor who comments upon groups of poems, each group containing its own "posie" or motto, usually in Latin, after each poem. There are several different mottoes, and the assumption was that each motto identified a different poet. *The Adventures* itself is presented through a series of letters and conversations between "F. J." and the editor, identified only as "G. T." On the surface, it seems to be the record of an adulterous affair between a Lady Elinor and F. J., as told to F. J.'s close friend, G. T., the editor. That such a format is simply a mask to disguise the fact that G. T. and F. J. are the same person is obvious, for the editor in telling the story pos-

120 GEORGE GASCOIGNE

sesses information he could have gained only by directly experiencing the affair himself.

The deceit apparently was also quite obvious to certain people in the sixteenth century, for Gascoigne was threatened with libelous action and was forced to rewrite the story. He changed the setting of the novel from the north of England to Italy; altered the names of the major characters, although still using the original names of the ladies during the bulk of the story; gave its authorship to a fictitious Italian, Bartello; and added a highly moral ending. Of course, he also excised the more licentious passages. In this form, *The Adventurers* was allowed to be printed; and it appeared with the expanded and altered 1575 edition, called simply *The Posies,* which acknowledged Gascoigne's authorship of the entire work.

The changes Gascoigne made served to mollify several separate sources of trouble. The first source, the people of the court whose reputations were involved, were content with the disguise of an Italian translation. The second source, the bishops, the moral censors of the country, had been disgusted by the open sexuality of the first edition; although they allowed the publication of the second edition, they effectively destroyed its chances of success, and with it the literary career of Gascoigne, a point he makes again and again in his later poems. A third source of trouble is more difficult to define. We feel, from reading the revised novel, that Gascoigne withdrew much of the humor and the satire found in the first edition. He is not so much the humorous self-critic, the deflator of romantic attitudes, or the ridiculer of conventional love poetry; instead, he is more moral, more severe, and, in an indefinable sense, older. In the 1573 edition—his first earnest attempt to achieve popularity— he had reached toward the court and fashionable society, only to be severely rebuffed. Never again did he write the strong, lighthearted poetry that characterizes this edition. His poems became increasingly introspective, pessimistic, and darkly critical. Paralleling F. J. himself, Gascoigne's first serious artistic involvement with the outside world brought only frustration and the start of a growing self-doubt.

II *The English Novel Tradition*

An important characteristic of *The Adventures* is its position in the history of the novel.[2] It is fruitless to argue whether Lyly's

Euphues, Deloney's *Jack of Newbury,* Nashe's *Unfortunate Traveller,* or Gascoigne's *The Adventures* can wholly claim the distinction of being the first true English novel. Each work has its merits; each its drawbacks. *Euphues,* for example, pays more attention to structure and balance than do the others, but these elements are hopelessly buried under the extravagant euphuistic style and are dug up only by tireless critics, not by the average close reader. Such points, both good and bad, may be shown for any sixteenth-century work of prose fiction; therefore, it is wiser to concentrate on those features of *The Adventures* which are significant in the development of the novel, and to avoid any dogmatic statement as to whether or not *The Adventures* is the first English novel.

The one feature above all others that makes *The Adventures* important is that it is a story of character exposure and change—often called "a psychological novel." The characters who are probed are F. J., Lady Elinor, and Mistress Frances. When F. J. first arrives at the country home of the Duke, he is a bright, self-centered, almost arrogant youth who is quite skilled in the graces of court life, but who is quite immature. The Duke had invited F. J. specifically to court his daughter, Frances, who is described by F. J. as "a virgin of rare chastitie, singular capacitie, notable modestie, and excellent beauty." Lady Elinor, who is married to the Duke's son, is also beautiful; but her beauty is a petulant, provocative kind that always focuses upon itself—and this selfishness is displayed through a long list of conquests, seduction for her being the triumph of her beauty over all opposing forces such as male ego, social and religious morality, and the competition of other women. Gascoigne adds to her character a strong element of lust which motivates her to extend her love affairs beyond the mere triumph of a sexual conquest. Elinor's two traits and their effect on two innocent people are what Gascoigne explores in the novel: her selfish and amoral desire for conquest, and her lust.

After the first evening's entertainment, F. J. is completely won by Elinor. He composes poems and riddles and he devises accidental private meetings to tell her of his great love; but his suit is unsuccessful until her paramour-secretary, his position unknown to F. J., leaves on a mission. Up to this point, Elinor simply toyed with F. J. to keep his attentions away from Mistress Frances. But now that her lust has no outlet, she turns to F. J.; and, employing her well-practiced methods, she quickly lets him "win" her.

At this point in the story, we see the depth, or lack of depth, of Elinor's character; we see the whole shallow character of F. J., but we know little about Frances. At first, Frances had tried to win F. J. with her gentility; but, when she realized that she was losing, her wit became sarcastic and she reacted like a little girl who pinches a little boy because he doesn't kiss her. However, as Elinor begins her seduction of F. J., Frances changes and becomes selfless and generous. We see this change first when she tries to warn F. J. of Elinor's true character. Then, as he loses his confidence just before the seduction, she actually tells him how to win Elinor, spies on them as they successfully consummate their love affair, and plays on him a lighthearted but rather symbolic trick involving the loss of his manhood. Through the duration of F. J.'s affair with Elinor, Frances is constantly his friend—entertaining him when he is depressed, giving him advice, diverting the Duke's suspicions, arranging meetings with Elinor. The answer to why she does all this is simple, yet tragic: she has fallen completely in love with F. J., and she must do only what one in love can—help the loved one in any way possible.

A powerful contrast between three types of love is now developed. Elinor loves only herself, and thus her love is destructive to those who love her, and distasteful to those who do not. F. J.'s infatuation is the second kind of love, and he is blind both to what true love is and to the destructive aspects of lust and self-love. Frances loves honestly and selflessly, and her love, the third kind, is a healing force throughout the novel. However, the tragedy of her love is that even at the moment of its greatest strength it has the power to change only one life, her own. That moment comes when Frances, highly moral, intelligent, and honest, discovers that F. J. has been discarded by Elinor in favor of the returned secretary. Knowing how despondent and, probably, physically sick he must be, she goes to F. J. several times to offer good advice and courtly entertainment. But as all this fails to cheer him, she offers herself in place of the lost Elinor. She does not ask for his love or for marriage; she simply wishes to console him in what she believes the most healing of all ways—to give him a new woman to replace the old one.

But F. J. rejects her; for, filled with self-pity and a feeble sense of outrage, he is almost wholly blind to the magnificent sacrifice offered him by Frances. She is willing to forget all the moral values of a lifetime because she loves him—a supreme gesture of love—and she is rejected by a petulant youth who scarcely has the grace to show her he is aware of her nobility. This scene could quite easily have been melodramatic, but Gascoigne handles the characters and the situation so adroitly that both are believable and realistic—indeed, even entertaining in the clever and sophisticated ways in which Frances broaches the proposal and F. J. rejects it. The offer is made most openly in the following scene: "By this time the sleeping houre aproched, & the Ladies prepared their departure, when as mistres *Fraunces* said unto *F. J.* Although percase I shal not do it so handsomly as your mistres, yit good *Trust* (quod she) if you vouchsafe it, I can be content to trim up your bed in ye best maner that I may, as one who would be as glad as she to procure your quiet rest. *F. J.* gave hir gret thanks desiring hir not to trouble hirself, but to let his man alone with that charge" (Prouty, 74). The obvious double entendre and J. F.'s blindness to it keep the scene from being mawkish or exaggerated.

To conclude the brief plot summary, F. J., shortly after his success with Elinor, loses her to her former lover through his own jealousy. He becomes increasingly bitter, but he finally composes several poems which show that, through his experience, he has gained some manly pride; and he rides from the manor a changed man. Elinor, after rejecting F. J., remains indifferent to him and quite satisfied with the resumption of her old love affair. She appears infrequently in the latter part of the novel, and then only to conflict with Frances who is strongly contemptuous of her sister-in-law, or to reply to F. J.'s accusation of unfaithfulness with all the arrogance of lust and selfishness in the words, "And if I did, what then?," which becomes the title of F. J.'s final poem. We see her finally as completely corrupt and destructive. Frances, who remains F. J.'s friend, helps him considerably to conquer his bitterness; but, when F. J. leaves, she becomes submerged in grief.

Character analysis and character development are a major focal point of *The Adventures*; and to achieve clarity, to insure that we understand the psychology of the people involved, Gascoigne uses symbols, short anecdotes, an allegory, poems, rid-

dles, questions, direct statements from the pseudoeditor, and
other more common narrative devices. The characters, with the
exception of F. J., speak in a consistent voice peculiar to themselves and are entirely predictable in their actions. The lesser
characters are all given believability. The Duke, for instance,
although genuinely hospitable, forces embarrassment on his
guests through his overemphasis on everyone's taking part in
the merriment. And Dame Pergo, an elderly woman, because
she had lost her lover in her youth, seems quite critical of both
F. J. and Frances; and, at times she takes a spiteful delight in
their misery. It is fair to say that, although the characters may be
regarded as types, with the exception of Frances, Gascoigne's
handling of them makes them come alive as vital parts of the
story he is telling.

III Satire

As has been indicated, F. J., unlike the others, does not speak
in a consistent voice peculiar to his character. He, rather, is an
exaggeration of a type character—the courtly lover—and the
exaggeration appears in two areas, in his speech and in his
actions. For example, in his actions F. J. appears to us to be
selfish, stupid, and anemic; but to the other characters he appears
to be just the opposite. His heart continually palpitates with
desire, depriving him of his appetite and sending him to his bed.
He keeps to his chamber for days at a time, he is unable to take
nourishment or entertainment, and he causes concern among the
others for his health—all because his desires for Elinor are un-
satisfied. He blushes; he at one time faints in Elinor's arms;
and he is continually embarrassed by Frances's knowing innuendo. Yet, to contrast to this mawkish behaviour, he shows his
excellent horsemanship and his graceful dancing; he exhibits
great self-assurance when he heals Elinor's nosebleed; and he
shows his skill at repartee and invention during several evenings'
entertainments. The exaggeration, then, lies in his excessive reactions to anything concerning love—specifically, his love toward
Elinor. On most other counts, he acts quite normally.

The second area is his speech. Nearly every time F. J. speaks,
his words are so stilted, so formal, so filled with compliment and
manners, so emptied of feeling—in short, so courtly—that, given
the situation, they provoke immediate laughter. For example,
as F. J. is on the brink of his first amorous experience with

Elinor, his words are: "Oh my deare Lady, when shall I be able with any desert to countervayle the least parte of this your bountifull goodnesse?" (Prouty, 69). The lady of course pays no attention to his words but proceeds directly to her goal. Later, when F. J. is in his chambers sick with the thought that Elinor is being unfaithful, Elinor comes to his bed to prove otherwise. In his joy, he swoons; but she revives him with various amorous devices; and, as she slips onto the bed beside him, F. J. says:

Mistresse, as for my maladie, it hath ben easely cured by your bountifull medicines applied: But I must confesse, that in receiving that guerison at your handes, I have ben constreined to fall into an Extasie, through the galding remembrance of myne own unworthines: Neverthelesse good Mistresse, since I perceive such fidelitie remayning betwene us, as that fewe wordes will perswade such trust as lovers ought to embrace, let these fewe wordes suffise to crave your pardon, and doe eftsones powre upon me (your unworthy servaunt) the haboundant waves of your accustomed clemency; for I must confesse, that I have so highly offended you, as (but your goodnesse surpasse the malice of my conceipts) I must remayne (and that right woorthely) to the severe punishment of my desertes: . . . (Prouty, 91)

This time even Elinor becomes impatient with him and they quarrel; and we suddenly see that all F. J.'s fine phrases are utterly empty, for, in a surge of immature self-righteousness and indignation, he rapes the lady. He does not act in lust; instead the dominant mood is selfish jealousy; and he spends the following hours in tortured self-doubt—not shamed by his act but worried that he may now have lost her for good. This rape scene, although the highest satiric point in the book, is also the moment of profoundest insight into F. J.'s character. We see that none of the highly idealistic sentiments of love which he has been writing and saying are of the slightest value to him. His all-important acts of love are determined by blind emotions and passions, not by publicly stated and socially accepted laws of conduct.

To see the satire, we must see F. J. and his society. F. J. presents the façade of courtier and gentleman to himself and to everyone around him. He knows the popular dances, his repartee is excellent, his swords- and horsemanship are good: he is the proper combination of knight and courtier. By following the rules of society, that is, by remaining within the courtly love tradition which had governed upper-class society for over four hundred years, F. J. quite honestly could expect to have secret, adulterous love affairs wherever he went in society. The rules were simple: he merely had to offer his services to a woman of the court, be her constant companion and entertainer, and remain absolutely discreet. The conversation between them would have to be about love as a noble and ideal force, capable of purifying the lovers and even, perhaps, immortalizing them. Then, if satisfied that her "servaunt" knew the rules of the game and if made secure by his complete discretion, the lady would bestow her favors upon him for as long as it was safe and mutually enjoyable. Gascoigne's society was able quite well to balance entirely different concepts of love—an idealized platonic love with an amoral physical love.[3]

Gascoigne satirizes this courtly love tradition mainly through the exaggeration of F. J.'s actions and speech. As pointed out above, both aspects of F. J. make him appear at once ridiculous and pathetic; yet, he is one of the two major figures in the story who act in the tradition. Gascoigne says through F. J. that the trappings of the courtly love tradition are absurd, old-fashioned, and serve to conceal buffoons and moral cowards, both of which F. J. is. The other figures also play a role in the satire. Through Elinor, Gascoigne says that the amoral basis of the tradition results in spiteful, lustful, and corrupt people, people whose sole end becomes self-pleasure. Gascoigne's most poignant point, made through Frances, is that a genuine, healthy love becomes smothered and withers in such an atmosphere of deceit and devotion to surface and immediate pleasures. The names given to each other by F. J. and Frances are symbolic of the higher ideals which are destroyed in the novel—she calls him "Trust," and he calls her "Hope." In the two editions, Frances is handled differently; in the first, she fades out of sight, and we feel only the loss of her kindness and good advice to F. J. In the second edition, she languishes for several months and then dies, a more moral and artificial ending, but also a more symbolic one.

Now we can see the importance of the rape scene: it shows the absolute inefficacy of the principles of courtly love. The lady is supposed to command the love of the gallant; he must be attentive to her least desire; to him, she is exalted above all living things. But what happens? Jealousy, greed, deceit, and lust are the emotions present; and the acts—the quarrel and rape

—debase both the lovers and the concept of love. In this moment of the highest possible achievement of courtly love—the lady coming to comfort her lover—the worst offenses against love take place; in fact, they are made inevitable by the very principles upon which the tradition is built. Rather than satirizing the parts of the tradition, Gascoigne strikes in this scene at its center. He brings to bear the ridicule resulting from F. J.'s exaggerated speech and actions plus the moral censure of the rape itself in order to emphasize what kind of a despicable caricature this debased love convention makes of a human being.

In his satire of the courtly love conventions, Gascoigne is not being essentially humorous. There are moments of great humor in the revealing of F. J.'s character, but we quickly become impatient with him and lose our amusement at his words and acts. The events of the story bear out Gascoigne's serious attitude. To the extent that a man can love honestly, he receives pain in return. Frances, who loves most, is hurt most, even dying in the second edition. F. J., although only infatuated, is still emotionally involved and feels considerable pain at being scorned. Elinor, of course, suffers not at all because she felt no love in any emotional sense of the word. Thus, the amoral Elinor triumphs in that she continues to live and have her own way as always; the idealistic Frances loses all and sickens with a broken heart; F. J., somewhere between the two women morally, rides from the scene in anger and bitterness. The pattern of the story is not essentially humorous.

IV *Poetry Criticism*

Yet, Gascoigne shows fine humor and wit in his criticism of contemporary poetic practices and in his willingness to make fun of his own poetic creations. *The Adventures* carries the story of F. J. in two ways, by narration and by poems. The poems form a record in the stages of F. J.'s progress toward love and toward maturity; in a sense, they punctuate the progress made at various stages in the story. Thus, when F. J. is first attracted to Elinor, his poems celebrate her beauty and his desire. After the conquest, the poems become boasting, crude, and possessive. When F. J. is rejected, they become the vehicle for his outraged feelings; at the end, they record what he has learned from the experience and what degree of maturity he has achieved. In this sense, they function quite well as a narrative device.

However, Gascoigne also uses the poems to attack the artificial and convention-ridden love poetry of his day. This attack
includes in its scope the writers of such poems and the critical
audience which gave them its approval, so that, even though
Gascoigne seems to aim primarily at himself, he certainly hit
and offended many influential men. This fact accounts to some
degree for the subsequent changes he made in the second edition—removing much of the critical material and changing the
order of the poems—and it also accounts for the change in tone
from the brisk and candid criticism of the first edition to the
subdued, indistinct criticism of the second. He literally excised
twelve to fifteen lines of critical text following some of his
poems in order to make the content more acceptable to prevailing literary tastes.

The critical remarks following the poems both defend his
composition and ridicule it. Each poem is supposedly composed
in the heat of passion, yet the editor-commentator is especially
far removed and objective. The resulting contrast in tone serves
to separate the criticism from the surrounding narrative and
to make it a separate dimension of the novel. The emphasis
usually is on propriety of diction and originality of invention;
and the direction of the major comments is to criticize the popular poetic practices, mainly the translating directly out of the
Italian and the copying of the Petrarchan style. After one long
poem extolling his love, supposedly delivered extemporaneously,
the pseudoeditor breaks into the mood of the passage with
the following comment: "These verses are more in number than
do stand with contentation of some judgements, and yit the occasion throughly considered, I can commend them with the
rest, for it is (as may be well termed) *continua oratio*, declaring
a full discourse of his first love: wherin (over and besides that
the Eypthetes are aptly applied, & the verse of it self pleasant
enough) . . ." (Prouty, 65). Thus, by apologizing for the poem,
he directly criticizes the critical tastes of those influential persons who decide on a poem's merit.

Today, one of the prevailing criticisms of Elizabethan lyric
poetry is that it is, in a sense, "formula" poetry—that it utilizes
the same form and subject matter over and over, with only
changes in phrasing and the poet's metrical adeptness to give
the poems any individuality. Among the lesser poets, it is often
very difficult to recognize the work one of from that of another.

The motivation for such poetry was most often to gain a reputation for the poet as a man with a nimble wit, a reputation which would help him reach worldly success.

In *The Adventures,* however, the motivation for the poems is exactly what it was meant to be in theory: to win the favors of a lady. Now, if we remember that the ultimate author, Gascoigne, basically is satirizing the whole courtly love tradition, we can see that in these satiric asides he is attacking one of the corrupt offshoots of the system. In the above-quoted passage, he goes on to say that, even though the poem was composed hastily and in rage, he still rejects it because of one unsuitable word. This exaggerated meticulousness serves to emphasize the fact that it is still a better poem than ones which are praised by accepted judges. Gascoigne feels that the corruption is that lyric poetry is accepted because it satisfies nonpoetical criteria, not because it is intrinsically good poetry.

The second half of Gascoigne's criticism is aimed at the criteria, which, according to Gascoigne, are determined by the Petrarchists. As we have seen, Gascoigne himself wrote many poems in this fashion, many of them quite good ones; but he always remained critical of Petrarchan conventions. Early in *The Adventures* all the poems are Petrarchan in subject matter and most of them in form; but, when F. J. wins and then loses his lady, the poems fall outside the conventions and Gascoigne's critical comments on them disappear. The reason, of course, is that the critical target, Petrarchanism, is gone.

Connected to the Petrarchan fashion was the popularity of translating Italian love poems, most of them basically Petrarchan, and Gascoigne touches upon this practice also. In the third poem of the novel, a sonnet, and in the comments following it, we can see what Gascoigne tries to do:

> Love, hope, and death, do stirre in me such strife,
> As never man but I led such a life,
> First burning love doth wound my hart to death,
> And when death comes at call of inward griefe
> Colde lingering hope, doth feede my fainting breath
> Against my will, and yeeldes my wound reliefe:
> So that I live, but yet my life is such,
> As death would never greve me halfe so much.
> No comfort then but only this I tast,
> To salve such sore, such hope will never want,

> And with such hope, such life will ever last,
> And with such life, such sorrows are not skant.
> Oh straunge desire, O life with torments tost
> Through too much hope, mine onely hope is lost.
>   Even *HE*   F. J.

This Sonet was highly commended, and in my judgement it deserveth no lesse, I have heard F. J. saye, that he borowed th'invention of an *Italian*: but were it a translation or invention (if I be Judge) it is both prety and pithy. (Prouty, 59-60)

The editor, G. T., thinks highly of this sonnet, and it is good in that it rehearses the standard Petrarchan conceits. It is to the point of the narrative except that, as G. T. says of another poem, it overstates the emotion. This overstatement fits perfectly the character of F. J. at this time; but F. J. himself is a caricature, and so his poetry, like himself, is held up to ridicule. This ridicule includes all the central clichés of Petrarchanism and the practice of adapting Italian poetry. As we know, Gascoigne champions English poetry and the English language as a vehicle for poetry in his important serious critical writings; but here he accomplishes the same end by ridiculing that which he believes to be harmful to English poetry.

We see, then, that Gascoigne attacks the courtly love tradition by putting the caricature F. J. in a real life setting and showing how inadequately F. J., as an extension of the tradition, reacts to events. He does the conventional things in conventional situations; yet, looked at realistically, his acts are absurd. He uses poetry as an instrument to achieve his desires, and it also becomes absurd. It is overly emotional and trite. In one scene, another basic flaw in such poetry is brought out—its fundamental impersonality. The poem "Beautie shut up thy shop" uses a traditional name for the heroine, Helen, instead of Elinor; and it inspires an argument between the two principals because Elinor is jealous that the poem is not about her though addressed to her. This quarrel proves to be the beginning of the end of the affair. The point which Gascoigne makes is that poetry which does not emanate entirely from the writer's own thought and emotions is useless for anything other than self-glorification. Petrarchan and other courtly love poetry, therefore, is essentially, and usually obviously, hypocritical. For, although the poem may be addressed to a particular lady, the compliments or passions declared in it are conventional and are very little concerned with the lady.

Following the break in relations with Elinor, F. J.'s poems become increasingly personal. Their lyric power increases, and they achieve an element of reality and immediacy far beyond the best of the previous poems. As he begins to see Elinor's character and his own foolish acts for what they are, he finally develops a sense of his own manhood; and he feels a consequent bubbling up of pride. He is quite an imperfect man, far below being able to accept the love of Frances; but he does finally see through the illusions of romantic love and is able to throw off the petty restrictions of the courtly conventions. His comments upon finding Elinor and her secretary in a compromising position show him developing a hard wit and an ability to separate the facts of lust from the feelings of love: "My losse is mine owne, and your gayne is none of yours, and soner can/ I recover my losse than you enjoy the gaine which you gape after" (Prouty, 104-5). His poetry, of course, reflects his growth, and at the end we see F. J. wounded and bleeding from his immature adventure into love, but healing. F. J. is not sophisticated and humorous about it, as Gascoigne is in telling the story; but he has learned. And his final poem, written as a response to Elinor's final admission of guilt, reflects the new wisdom. In it, we are shown both the degree of change which has occurred, and the distance his poetic composition has come from his early Petrarchan sonnets:

> And if I did what then?
> Are you agreev'd therfore?
> The Sea hath fishe for every man,
> And what would you have more?
>
> Thus did my Mistresse once,
> Amaze my mind with doute:
> And popt a question for the nonce,
> To beate my braynes about.
>
> Wherto I thus replied,
> Eche fisherman can wishe,
> That all the Sea at every tyde,
> Were his alone to fishe.
>
> And so did I (in vaine,)
> But since it may not be:

Let such fishe there as find the gaine,
And leave the losse for me.

And with such lucke and losse,
I will content my selfe:
Till tydes of turning time may tosse,
Such fishers on the shelfe.

And when they sticke on sands,
That every man may see:
Then will I laugh and clappe my hands,
As they do now at mee.
                              F.J.
                     (Prouty, 105)

In this poem, Gascoigne's typically pessimistic, ironic voice comes strongly through. F. J.'s experiences have finally given his poems individuality and a quality of pertinence that his formal courtly poetry could never achieve.

In one sense, unfortunately *The Adventures* fails as satire. We see Frances and Elinor and, most importantly, F. J. too closely and know them too well not to react to them emotionally. In spite of F. J.'s obvious faults, perhaps because of them, we come to understand him and to join him in his climb to maturity. He gains dignity as he learns that pure sexuality destroys all the finer elements of human nature, such as pride in his manhood or the gentleness and grace that Elinor lost in her drive for self-satisfaction. Unfortunately, this dignity loses for him his status as a satiric figure; but it gives the dimension of character development and growth to the novel.

Whether *The Adventures* is basically an autobiographical novel, as several of his critics have claimed, or is an example of the popular *roman à clef*, a major motivation for this story is certainly to show the forces acting on F. J. which made him so foolish and to attack them in some way; and it is here that the satire comes into play. But Gascoigne had to attack a whole way of life, one which contained both good and evil and which was too complex to allow easy separation of the two. Thus, F. J. never rejects the courtly love tradition; but Gascoigne, who is in a sense F. J. grown up, can at least find fault with it. F. J. writes Petrarchan love poems which are not at all bad poems, but his best and most honest poems are outside the Petrarchan tradition. The Petrarchan poems allow the courtier to display his wit, but the nonconventional lyric poems allow the poet to convey his emotions. Also, in Frances we see a paradox which simply must be accepted: she contrasts completely with the debased courtly love tradition, but she cannot make her nobler and more honestly felt emotional love more attractive than the lustful sexuality of Elinor.

In a sense, Gascoigne says that F. J. is blameless; society is at fault. F. J. gave way to the strong superficial desires because his world encouraged such actions, while, at the same time, it inhibited the growth of a deeper kind of love. Gascoigne knows the faults of his society; he rehearses them many times in his poems. Similarly, he knows his own weaknesses. *The Adventures* attempts to show what happens to that weak man in that imperfect world.

V *Prose Style*

The sophisticated tone of *The Adventures,* which adds greatly to our enjoyment of the novel, is essential in establishing the great contrast between F. J. and the narrator: one between immaturity and sophistication. The one conclusion we must *not* adopt is that F. J., having learned his lesson, rides away to lead a highly moral life of honor and love. Even the rigidly revised ending of the second edition does not suggest that; it could not, without damaging the structure of the story. F. J. eventually evolves into someone like Gascoigne himself, and Gascoigne is neither rigidly moral nor high-minded. Rather, he is a man of the world, survivor of a number of love affairs, and quite able to see both the humor and the tragedy in all human relationships; and to this position F. J. is heading. F. J. is made to see himself and his desires in all their nakedness; he is made to suffer the loss of Elinor so that he could break the bubble of immature egoism and see the world outside himself in its true colors; and he must reject Frances and, thus, love because she is superior to him. She watched him lose his manhood; she helped him to see through Elinor; therefore, to become his own man again, he must also be rid of Frances. He did not love her, but he became sympathetic to her love; and we see in the brief reference to their parting—"I could wade much further, as to declare his departure, what thenkes he gave to his *Hope,*&c. Yet I will cease"—that he was strong enough to express it. F. J. has learned, and he is on his way to becoming the man the author already is.

We can discover the personality of the author in the style of prose before us. We see immediately that the author is witty. He enjoys making puns, and he is clever at devising riddles for the characters to toy with. These are facets of a skilled courtier, one who has listened to much repartee and perhaps contributed his own. Another mark of a courtier is the ready compliment to a lady, and the story abounds with them. Also, the skilled courtier frequently passes off phrases in other languages, and Gascoigne does this often; for example, he refers to the first kisses between F. J. and Elinor as *Bezo las manos* and *zuccado dez labros*. But the most distinctive characteristic of Gascoigne is his great use of innuendoes, particularly of ribald ones. These occur throughout the story, but a few examples indicate their flavor and suggest the complexity of parts of the story.

At one time after the seduction, Elinor's husband returns. This event does not hamper the affair; instead, F. J. and the husband become good friends. F. J. at this time is perfectly arrogant. On a deer hunt, the husband asks if he may blow F. J.'s hunting horn; but, upon receiving it, he is unable to blow, or wind, it; and the scene calls forth the following response:

Quod *F. J.* although I have not ben over lavishe of my comming hitherto, I woulde you shoulde not doubt but that I can tell howe to use a horne well enough, and yet I may little do if I maye not lende you a horne, and therewithall took his Beugle from his necke, and lent it to the Knight, who making in unto the houndes, gan assaye to rechate: but the horne was to hard for him to wynde, whereat *F. J.* tooke pleasure, and sayde to him selfe, blowe tyll thou breake that: I made thee one within these fewe dayes, that thou wilt never cracke whiles thou livest. And hereupon (before the fal of the Buck) devised this sonet following, . . .

> As some men say there is a kind of seed
> Will grow to hornes if it be sowed thick:
> Wherwith I thought to trye if I could breed
> A brood of buddes, well sharped on the prick:
> And by good proofe of learned skill I found,
> (As on some speciall soyle all seedes best frame)
> So jelouse braynes doe breed the battle ground,
> That best of all might serve to beare the same.
> Then sought I foorth to find such supple soyle,
> And cald to mynd thy husband had a brayne,

> So that percase, by travayll and by toyle,
> His fruitfull front might turne my seed to gayne:
> And as I groped in that ground to sowe it,
> Start up a horne, thy husband could not blow it.
>
> *F. J.*
> (Prouty, 78-79)

When we look beneath the surface, the number of double and triple meanings is endless. Besides the obvious reference to cuckoldry, there are phallic meanings and references to sexual performance underlying the entire passage in humorous and profuse complexity.

Another but more controlled innuendo appears near the end of the story. At this point, Frances attempts to intercede with Elinor for F. J. and discovers Elinor and the secretary in a very embarrassing posture. The author's figurative description of the scene is humorously effective:

And in very deed, it fell out that the *Secretary* having bin of long time absent, & therby his quils & pennes not worn so neer as they were wont to be, did now prick such faire large notes, that his Mistres liked better to sing faburden under him, than to descant any longer uppon *F. J.* playne song: ... Dame *Fraunces* came into hir chamber uppon such sudeyn as shee had like to have marred all the musick. Wel thei conveied their clifs as closely as they could, ...   (Prouty, 93)

A final example of the type of innuendo which Gascoigne uses has at least some narrative justification in that it stems from the nature of the secretary's position in the household. F. J. is just beginning to hold a possessive, boastful attitude toward Elinor before the seduction, and his emotion finds its outlet in deriding his competition:

This manling, this minion, this slave, this secretary, was nowe by occasion rydden to London forsothe: and ... he thought good now to smyte while the yron was hotte, and to lend his Mistresse suche a penne in hir Secretaries absence, as he should never be able at his returne to amende the well writing thereof, ...   (Prouty, 58)

At the end of the story, finding himself replaced by the secretary, F. J. returns to the same consistent imagery as these comments indicate. Throughout the story, F. J. allows no other apprehension of the man to color his opinion of him. He sees him solely as a sexual competitor.

The resulting picture of the author at first seems rather crude, but we have to remember that Gascoigne must balance a number of things in his work. He is writing satire, he is teaching a moral lesson, and he is showing character and character change. The continuing contrast between the struggling F. J. and the heavily ironic tone of the author is one way these elements are held together. Also, Gascoigne is writing for an audience that he feels is to some extent cynical and jaded, and the sexual humor is one way to entertain them. But, above all, he is trying to create real people; and the people at F. J.'s social level are fully aware of the ways of the world. Dame Pergo's long story on young love may be told idealistically; but Pergo herself, now an older person, relishes her lewd innuendo when she tells Frances of F. J.'s fall from favor. Frances, the representative of honest love, is most human when, giving in to a rather coarse quirk of humor, she steals F. J.'s naked sword after his first seduction, a most obvious phallic symbol. Gascoigne, through his innuendo, is showing his understanding of the people of that or any time. He brings to his readers, then and now, a rather more sophisticated love of humor than we get from the Petrarchists or from the popular romances. Too often the Petrarchists' poetry is sensual or lewd without the balancing effect of humor. But Gascoigne employs hard and sophisticated wit; and, if the basic material is coarse, the handling of it allows the most prudish of us to laugh, even though only privately.

CHAPTER 8

The Three Plays

WHEN we read Gascoigne's plays, we are immediately aware that the first two plays, *The Supposes* and *Jocasta,* are translations and vary considerably from his last play, *The Glasse of Governement,* which is original. The two translated plays were done party as exercises, partly as experiments; and their form and content reflect the purposes of their original authors. *The Glasse of Governement,* however, handles several themes which we now recognize as arising from Gascoigne's own early experiences, and it treats them with a certain grim irony that gives the play a strength which the others lack. The first two plays, *The Supposes* and *Jocasta,* were translated and produced in 1566, while Gascoigne was attending Gray's Inn for the second time. He translated *The Supposes* from Ariosto by himself and Euripides's *Jocasta* from the Italian playwright Dolce with the help of Francis Kinwelmershe. *The Supposes* holds the unique distinction of being the first Italian comedy to be translated into English and also of being the first English play to use prose dialogue. In both respects, *The Supposes* is important to English drama. *Jocasta* stands as the first Greek tragedy to appear on an English stage. So we can see that the time Gascoigne spent in Gray's Inn was fruitful; indeed, he and his companions for a few years were the center of English drama. They wrote and acted in plays that helped form the tastes of their age and which influenced the shape of the drama to come, both in the content of the drama—the Italian comic mode and the Greek-Senecan tragic mode—and in the form—prose dialogue, adaptation of coherent scene divisions, Senecan characteristics, and others.[1]

The Glasse of Governement, the third and original play, was written after Gascoigne returned from the Dutch wars; it shows, in contrast to the other plays, a change in his mood. He was no longer lighthearted and full of illusions; he was wiser and, to some extent, regretful of the lost time of his young life. This change appears, first of all, in his choice of a recognized form

for his drama, rather than an experimental one as in his earlier
ones. But, second, the intent of the play is to teach morals, to
demonstrate the wisdom of authority as contrasted to the foolish-
ness of inexperience. The play is not successful partly because of
the gravity in which Gascoigne approaches the theme. But
there are aspects in it, as in the others, which make us wish he
had given more time to the drama and less, perhaps, to the court.

I The Supposes

Gascoigne's first play, *The Supposes*, a translation of Ariosto's
play, is an example of "New Style" Italian comedy. The characters and situations are conventional, and the language is for the
most part refined. This style contrasts sharply with plays such
as William Stevenson's *Gammer Gurton's Needle*, which imitated
many aspects of Latin comedy and relied considerably on coarse
language and vulgar wit for its success. Although the material
of *The Supposes* is far removed from that which forms the substance of his work, Gascoigne accomplished several things in
the play: he avoids coarseness and eroticism and emphasizes
the moral positions of the characters; he utilizes the humor and
absurdity of the situation rather than the eroticism inherent in
it; and he develops a form of euphuistic dialogue that is remarkable in its grasp of the techniques perfected over a decade later
by Lyly. For example, in the same way that Euphues argues
love policies to himself, so does Polynesta's lover argue to himself:

Hard hap had I when I first began this unfortunate enterprise: . . .
thinking that as shevering colde by glowing fire, thurst by drinke,
hunger by pleasant repasts, and a thousande suche like passions finde
remedie by their contraries, so my restlesse desire might have founde
quiet by continuall contemplation. But alas, I find that only love
is unsaciable: for as the flie playeth with the flame till at last she
is cause of her own decay, so the lover that thinketh with kissing
and colling to content his unbrideled apetite, is commonly seene the
only cause of his owne consumption. . . . I reape the fruites of my
desire: yet as my joyes abounde, even so my paines encrease. I fare
like the covetous man, that having all the world at will, is never
yet content: the more I have, the more I desire. . . . I know she
loveth me best of all others, but what may that prevaile when
perforce she shal be constrained to marie another? Alas, the pleasant
tast of my sugred joyes doth yet remaine so perfect in my remem-

brance, that the least soppe of sorow seemeth more soure than gal in my mouth. If I had never knowen delight, with better contentation might I have passed these dreadful dolours.... (Cunliffe, I, 197)

From this quotation, we can perceive something of Erostrato's character; but we also can see the action of the play being rehearsed.

As we might expect of Italian comedy, the plot situation is quite complex, whereas the plot action is relatively simple. Before the play opens, Erostrato, a Sicilian attending school in Ferrara, has fallen in love with the gentlewoman, Polynesta. In order to gain access to her, Erostrato has assumed the identity of his servant, Dulipo, and taken a position as servingman to her father, Damon. After bribing the nurse, Balia, to speak in his favor, Erostrato becomes Polynesta's lover; but he, of course, reveals his noble identity to his beloved. At this point the play begins. Cleander, an elderly doctor, wants Polynesta for his wife. To counter this suitor, Erostrato has his servant Dulipo, who is masquerading as Erostrato, also make suit for Polynesta. As Cleander has more money to offer, Erostrato's only device is to bring in a false father for the false Erostrato to make an even larger settlement—a scheme that fails when the real father suddenly arrives and unmasks Dulipo. Also at this time, Damon discovers Polynesta's indiscretion and claps Erostrato, a supposed servant, into a dungeon. However, the parasite Pasyphilo helps clear up the confusion, the three elderly men—Damon, Cleander, and Erostrato's father—come to an agreement, and the play ends happily.

The success of the play depends much more on the situation than on the characters. The characters are stock figures in Italian comedy—two young lovers, two greedy old men, a two-faced servant, a faithful servant, a corruptible nurse, an interfering old crone, and several low-life comic figures. None of these is on stage long enough to be a protagonist; indeed, all of them, except Erostrato's father, are guilty of one or another crime: Erostrato seduces Polynesta and deceives society at large; Polynesta loses her honor quite willingly; her father, Damon, wishes to sell her to the highest bidder; old Cleander is apparently fired by lust; and Dulipo, the faithful servant, is living a fraudulent life and is forced to renounce the master who once saved his life.

As is usual with stock figures, there is little attempt at depth of characterization. Erostrato, rather than capturing our sympathy, simply sums up past events when he says:

O howe often have I thoughte my selfe sure of the upper hande herein? but I triumphed before the victorie. And then how ofte againe have I thoughte the fielde loste? Thus have I beene tossed nowe over, nowe under, even as fortune list to whirle the wheele, neither sure to winne nor certayne to loose the wager. (Cunliffe, I, 212)

Polynesta, the center around which all the action moves, speaks only in the opening scene and does not appear onstage again until the end of the play. Dulipo, masquerading as Erostrato, is perhaps the most convincing character, for his position is completely untenable, and we feel his growing confusion and fear as events close in on him. Of the clowns, Pasyphilo is the most consistent with his ravenous appetite, yet he commands some admiration as a gourmet and leads directly to Greedy in Massinger's *A New Way To Pay Old Debts*.

The most puzzling lost opportunity to develop character comes when Erostrato's seduction of Polynesta is discovered by her father and Erostrato is thrown into a dungeon. We would expect speeches worthy of Euphues from Erostrato, or at least words of despair; but he is silent from this point until the last scene. Instead, we hear Damon, the father, airing his griefs in a long soliloquy:

My daughter is defloured, and I utterly dishonested: how can I then wype that blot off my browe? and on whom shall I seeke revenge? . . . O *Polynesta*, full evill hast thou requited the clemencie of thy carefull father: and yet to excuse thee giltlesse before God, and to condemne thee giltie before the worlde, I can count none other but my wretched selfe the caytife and causer of all my cares. . . . It is too true, that of all sorowes this is the head source and chiefe fountaine of all furies: the goods of the world are incertain, the gaines to be rejoyced at, and the losse not greatly to be lamented: only the children cast away, cutteth the parents throate with the knife of inward care, which knife will kill me surely, I make none other accompte.   (Cunliffe, I, 213-15)

Selfish though Damon is, Polynesta's sin has made him realize his own shortcomings.

The dialogue is witty, and the play moves rapidly into its complications. But the success of the play lies directly on its structure, and in this respect Ariosto simply plays upon the familiar

and successful theme of young lovers struggling to get together
against the desires of one or two old men and, to some extent
society. The twists in this play are the many cases of mistaken
identities (the reason for the title of the play by the way), and
they are explained by Gascoigne in "The Prologue":

But understand, this our Suppose is nothing else but a mystaking
or imagination of one thing for an other. For you shall see the master
supposed for the servant, the servant for the master: the freeman for
a slave, and the bondslave for a freeman: the stranger for a well
knowen friend, and the familiar for a stranger. (Cunliffe, I, 188)

False identity is the key to the play; critical moments arise when
the various characters learn of the duplicity and when Erostrato's
father comes looking for his noble son, only to find a servingman
in his place. The one case of unknown identity which surprises
audience and characters alike is Dulipo, who is really Cleander's
lost son.

As I have observed earlier, part of the play's importance lies
in the Italian source. It brought to the scholars, nobles, and gal-
lants a new, sophisticated comedy, not yet tainted by the eroticism which haunted such comedy during the following century
and a half and which finally destroyed it. In *The Supposes*, the
erotic elements are, however, present: an old man's lust for a
young, beautiful girl; a pandering nurse; a demure but sexually
permissive heroine; and a disguised nobleman who enjoys the
heroine almost at will. However, the play concentrates on the
problems faced by the two young lovers, not of how to satisfy
their desires (there they have no problems), but of how to
overcome the greater fortune of old Cleander so that they can
marry.

The play emphasizes the position of each character rather than
his deeper emotions. Erostrato's speech, quoted above in part,
explains his position intellectually. Damon's long soliloquy points
out precisely why he feels injured: the loss of his daughter's
honor means not only that his reputation suffers and that he will
not receive money for her hand but also that she cannot hope to
live in the noble world to which she had been bred. Cleander's
speech, when he discovers Dulipo to be his lost son, explains
why he suddenly no longer desires Polynesta. Apparently, he only
wanted an heir for his fortunes and saw Polynesta as the most
desirable mother. In the light of this explanation, all the others'
insulting remarks about his lust and greed seem suddenly shal-

low, although we cannot help but feel that the author is white-washing Cleander to some extent.

In this way, by concentrating on the intellectual aspects of their positions, the play avoids the traps of sensuality and eroticism which this type of situation comedy can so easily fall into, and it sets a tone of critical objectivity which influenced English comedy for nearly seventy-five years.

II Jocasta: *A Political Exercise*

The story of Jocasta, mother and wife of Oedipus, is less well known to us than the story of her husband-son Oedipus or her daughter Antigone. However, the narrative raises several questions which vitally interested Elizabethan artists and which were directly relevant to England—the question of an heir to the throne, the dangers of civil war, and the more eternal problems of ambition, hate, pride, and the workings of fate. Both *Oedipus Rex* and *Antigone* were known; and, by the end of the sixteenth century, their purer dramatic character was realized. But they are essentially studies in tyranny and in man against fate, and they did not fulfill the political requirements of the 1560's. Gascoigne's *Jocasta*, with its emphasis upon the public ruin brought about by private ambition, did.

To a modern audience, *Jocasta* comes across as an unsuccessful play. Too many major characters have deep-seated problems which, as they are brought to light one by one, reduce the emotional unity of the drama, Jocasta, her two sons, Antigone, and Creon are all focused upon at some time during the play. At the play's start, Jocasta is already reeling under the guilt of having been wife to her own son; and the conditions of Oedipus's disgrace—blindness and internment—are continually before her. Also, her two sons (by Oedipus) have quarreled over the rule of Thebes, and one has raised a Greek army to win Thebes from the other. The inevitability of the death of at least one of them increases Jocasta's grief. In her attempt to create peace, she brings them face to face before the battle, thus initiating the major action of the play.

Eteocles and Polinices, her sons, were to share the rule of Thebes by ruling on alternate years. Eteocles, being first to rule, became ambitious and usurped the kingship entirely to himself, forcing Polinices to seek aid from other cities to restore his right. Polinices, the favored one of the women, is referrred to as "sweet" and "gentle Polinices" by Antigone particularly. In the battle before Thebes, Eteocles's army is victorious; but he decides to press the victory and challenges Polinices to single combat. Both are killed; and Jocasta, overcome by the sight, kills herself. Antigone throughout the play has strongly favored Polinices, and we see the extent of Eteocles's treachery mainly through her speeches. After the battle she attempts to bury Polinices, but is prevented by Creon, Jocasta's brother, who assumes kingship upon Eteocles's death. She thwarts Creon's wish that she marry his son and accompanies the now-banished Oedipus into exile at the play's end.

Creon, the other major figure, is a bit more complex. In the opening "argument" of the play, Creon is called "King, the type of Tyranny"; but his tyranny consists only in refusing Polinices burial and in banishing Oedipus. However, Creon has long desired the kingship; Antigone, we find, is more fearful of him than of Eteocles:

> Besides all this, a certaine jelousie,
> Lately conceyvde (I know not whence it springs)
> Of *Creon*, my mothers brother, appaules me much,
> Him doubt I more than any danger else.
> (Cunliffe, I, 256-57)

Yet, when the blind seer Tyresias tells Creon that he must sacrifice his son Meneceus in order to become king, Creon refuses and is genuinely grieved when Meneceus takes his own life to save Thebes.

Gascoigne's play, in fact, contains many contradictions which are posed rather than answered. On the political level, both brothers share blame for the tragic war. Eteocles, of course, committed the first offense by usurping the throne in a tyrannical fashion; his crime is compounded by his increasing hatred of Antigone and Oedipus. But, as Eteocles points out, Polinices is bringing foreign troops to wage war against his own people; he is willing to destroy Thebes so that he may rule it. To compound the crime, Polinices has taken a foreign wife—that is, made a foreign alliance—to raise his army for such an attack. Thus, both brothers are guilty. Certainly Polinices has been wronged, but is he justified in destroying his city, in causing many innocent deaths, to right his own personal wrong? The comment implicit in the English version is that death and destruction are the necessary results of pride and ambition. The question of right and wrong is superficial. Rather, English lords and politicians should learn the lesson of history and avoid the original causes.

Another problem, one which has theological overtones, is the guilt attached to Jocasta. I say "theological" rather than "philosophical" because the English dramatists did not show much understanding of Greek concepts of destiny and free will until Marlowe's time in the 1590's. Generally, the vicissitudes of man's fate were blamed on the turning Wheel of Fortune, as the translators' additions to the play demonstrate. However, the unfairness of Jocasta's position, that of being punished for a sin of which she was completely unaware when she committed it, brought forth some objections similar to the ones Milton used to ameliorate Adam's guilt in *Paradise Lost*. In the original play, Jocasta's guilt and grief must remain unmitigated even though she is essentially a gentle and loving woman who refuses to blame any other person for the evil besetting Thebes. Tyresias tells us of the extent of her guilt when speaking to Creon:

> The incest foule, and childbirth monstruous
> Of *Jocasta*, so stirres the wrath of Jove
> This citie shall with bloudy channels swimme,
> And angry *Mars* shall overcome it all
> With famine, flame, rape, murther, dole and death:
> These lustie towres shall have a headlong fall,
> These houses burnde, and all the rest be razde,
> And soone be sayde, here whilome *Thebes* stoode.
> (Cunliffe, I, 287)

Yet, the English version, through Creon, makes the distinction that her sin was unwilled:

> O *Jocasta*, miserable mother,
> What haplesse ende thy life alas hath hent?
> Percase the heavens purveyed had the same,
> Moved therto by the wicked wedlocke
> Of *Oedipus* thy sonne yet might thy scuse
> But justly made, that knewe not of the crime.
> (Cunliffe, I, 310)

Such a sentiment could only arise from a theology which presupposes punishment in another world, not the Grecian theology which poses the inexplicable problem of life rather than death. This one statement, unimportant in a dramatic context, seems to echo the Anglican position in opposition to the Puritan dogma of Election: that certain men are doomed to damnation from birth and that others are elected to salvation in spite of the lives each may lead. To an Anglican, Jocasta's crime could not lead to her damnation because her crime was not self-willed; and the misery and grief in her life are attributable to the turns of fortune which all mankind must bear. It was for later dramatists such as Webster, Tourneur, and Shakespeare to realize the greater dramatic and poetic possibilities of the Greek tragic view.

The question of why the men of Gray's Inn produced Jocasta rather than, perhaps, *Oedipus Rex* may be answered on several grounds. *Jocasta* plays upon the evils of civil war and the troubles inherent in the breakdown of ordered authority. Remembering that the ravages of the War of the Roses were still apparent in England and that Queen Elizabeth was unmarried and thus had no apparent heir, we can understand how concerned Englishmen were over the orderly succession of the throne. Sackville's and Norton's *Gorboduc*, produced at Gray's Inn a few years earlier, portrayed the evils of a divided kingship. Statesmen, scholars, and artists all besieged the queen to marry in order to avoid civil disorder in the event of her death. All were afraid of the results of an unscrupulous ambition and were aware of the force the throne held to offset it. *Jocasta*, if nothing more, was another appeal to settle the issue of succession by demonstrating the lesson of history. In marginal notes and poetic appendices to the play, the view of *Jocasta* as a "mirrour for magistrates" is urged upon the reader and spectator.

Another reason the play was chosen lies in its Senecan flavor. To the Inns of Court dramatists, Seneca offered new and exciting drama techniques, and they imitated him in such plays as *Gorboduc* and translated him directly. Senecan characteristics are well known, but it is worthwhile noting those used in *Jocasta*. The "dumme shewe" is the first characteristic offered to the audience. In it, the actors pantomime an action, such as a pope removing his crown and robes and putting on armor. In *Jocasta* there are five dumb shows. The one preceding the third act gives a good example of how elaborate they could become:

Before the beginning of this .iii. Act did sound a very dolefull noise of cornettes, during the which there opened and appeared in the stage a great Gulfe. Immediatly came in .vi. gentlemen in their dublets & hose, bringing upon their shulders baskets full of earth and threwe them into the Gulfe to fill it up, but it would not so close up nor be filled. Then came the ladyes and dames that stoode by, throwing in their cheynes & Jewels, so to cause it stoppe up and close it selfe: but when it would no so be filled, came in a knighte with his sword drawen, armed at all poyntes, who walking twise or thrise about it, & perusing it, seing that it would nether be filled with earth nor with their Jewells and ornaments, after solempne reverence done to the gods, and curteous leave taken of the Ladyes and standers by, sodeinly lepte into the Gulfe, the which did close up immediatly: betokning unto us the love that every worthy person oweth unto his native countrie, by the historye of *Curtius,* who for the lyke cause adventured the like in Rome. This done, blind *Tyresias* the devine prophete led in by hys daughter, and conducted by *Meneceus* the son of *Creon,* entreth by the gates *Electrae,* and sayth as followeth. (Cunliffe, I, 283)

The appeal of the dumb shows to Englishmen stems from the long tradition of mumming. However, it was through Seneca's influence that it became a major dramatic technique, one used with great effect by later Renaissance dramatists such as John Webster.

Another device is the long set speech, such as Jocasta delivers at the beginning of the play and the one Nuntius gives near the play's end. Such speeches allow the full exploitation of the playwright's rhetorical ability; and in the hands of Marlowe, this characteristic developed into a superb dramatic instrument used by all the major dramatists. It is also a major factor in the development of the soliloquy, to which Renaissance drama owes much.

Seneca also inspired interest in violence and horror. Because Senecan plays were written to be read, not to be acted, bloody or horrible events occurred away from the action of the play and then were described to the reader in great detail by a "Nuntius." In this way, rhetoric conveyed the desired impact of violence and terror to the reader who otherwise would not be able to visualize it from reading the bare dialogue. In *Jocasta,* we see this interest reflected in the speech of the Nuntius describing the battle and the deaths of Jocasta and her two sons. One of the dramatic weaknesses of *Jocasta,* as a play made to be acted on stage, is the large proportion of reported action as against staged action. However, subsequent dramatists learned from these early experiments and brought violence and horror onstage in increasing degrees, turning their rhetoric into other areas.

III   The Glasse of Governement

Gascoigne's only original play, *The Glasse of Governement,* is a highly moralistic drama illustrating the "prodigal son" theme.[2] Since the play was written in 1575 after Gascoigne had spent time soldiering in the Netherlands, it undoubtedly was influenced by Dutch plays on the same subject; but Gascoigne's contributions to this type of play are original and interesting. The typical prodigal-son story tells of a young man who leaves his family and spends his inheritance in riotous living. He descends into ruin and ill health, and he loses all his fortune. His family, however, forgives him and takes him back into the fold. The essential parts of the story are the young, proud, undisciplined son and the forgiving father. If we regard the youth as mankind, the father as Christ, and the family as the Christian community, we have the substance of the Christian moral.

Both on the Continent and in England, the Christian story is twisted somewhat because humanist playwrights focused on techniques of education. Prodigality became the result of an undisciplined mind; and, to humanist dramatists to whom theories of education were of primary concern, a prodigal-son play offered the most appropriate setting for discussions of proper educational methods. The emphasis on forgiveness, repentance, and grace was considerably less pronounced. The inherent drama of pride, despair, and salvation was overlooked, and the plays for the most part resembled moral sermons and pedagogical essays. Although both of these characteristics are apparent in *The Glasse of Governement,* Gascoigne added to the play dramatic qualities which he had learned while translating Ariosto and Euripides. These additions include conventional scene divisions which dictate that the onstage actors leave naturally at the scene's close; logical act divisions following the five-act structure; the use of a subplot and comic figures; the more complex technique of paralleling characters on different dramatic levels; the establishment of plausibly motivated situations and characters. I do not intend to discuss all of these aspects, but certain ones clearly indicate Gascoigne's important position in breaking away from the trite approach to this theme and in making it acceptable material for the drama.

Gascoigne's play is concerned with the careers of the sons of two families, Phylautus and Phylomusus in one family, and Phylosarchus and Phylotimus in the other. The two elder sons, Phylautus and Phylosarchus, with their desire for experience and their weariness with instruction, contrast to the two younger ones, Phylomusus and Phylotimus, who study diligently and do the tasks assigned them by their tutor, Gnomaticus. The older brothers' boredom is given relief by Lamia, a harlot, who becomes the catalyst to their rebellious acts. When Lamia's influence is discovered by the two fathers, all four sons are sent away to the university at Douai. Once there, the two elder sons leave school entirely and go their separate ways: Phylautus, eventually executed for robbery; and Phylosarchus, whipped and banished for fornication. The two younger brothers, who complete their education honorably, accept favorable positions in the community. There is an attempt by both the younger brothers and the fathers to save the errant sons. The fathers forgive their sons and send a servant, Fidus, to bring them home. The younger brother, Philotimus, pleads to save Phylosarchus from whipping. The interesting twist on the prodigal-son theme is that, although the fathers forgive the prodigals, they still receive the severest penalties for their crimes.

The characters of the harlot Lamia, Pandarina her "aunt," and her gentleman helpers, Dick Droom and Eccho, add considerable substance to the play. Lamia is quite a sympathetic character; she is, like the two elder brothers, rebelling against a restrictive, moralistic society. She says:

if I could have bene contented to be so shutte up from sight and speech of such as like me, I might have lived gallantly and well provided with my mother, who (though I say it) is a good old Lady in *Valentia*, but when I sawe that I must weare my good apparell alwayes within doores, and that I must passe over my meales without company, I trussed up my Jewelles in a casket, and (being accompanyed with my good Auntie here) I bad *Valentia* farewell, for I had rather make hard shifte to live at lyberty, then enjoy great riches in such a kind of emprisonment.   (Cunliffe, II, 23-24)

The final point in this speech is the basic irony of the play and certainly one of the central ironies of Gascoigne's life: life does not offer freedom and riches both; a young person must give up

one. Unfortunately, the society frowned on the value of freedom
for a young person; for such freedom led to excesses which led
to degeneration. Thus, a youth choosing to go his own way was
almost always severed from his family. Gascoigne's own youth
contained many elements of prodigality, and in many respects
Lamia's career is like his. Lamia's mistake is to accept the advice
of Pandarina too easily; but Lamia, young, attractive, willful,
wishes to have some fun out of life. Thus, her punishment, which
is three days on the "cucking stoole" and banishment, seems a
bit too harsh even though she did play a part in starting the two
elder brothers on the road to their destruction.

The play turns on a series of parallels or contrasts. The obvious
and unexceptional contrast is between the good and the bad
sons; but the more subtle parallel is between the bad sons and
Lamia. She has already rejected established authority and
morality, and they do so during the course of the play. Their
reasons are the same: boredom with accepted social roles and a
desire to pursue their own interests. None of the three carries
any hard feelings toward his parent: indeed, Lamia even says,
"I might have lived gallantly and well provided with my mother,
who (though I say it) is a good old Lady in *Valentia.*" It is
rather that, like many young people, they are stifled by parental
authority and must get away.

In the context of the play, their decisions and actions are evil
because they conflict with society's laws. The two sons are for-
given by their fathers but are cruelly punished by society, but
Lamia finds no forgiveness from any side. Her position, in fact,
causes the Servus, a police officer, some difficulty as he admits
to the two fathers: "and though I desire (as much as you) to
see them condingly corrected, yet with out proofe of some
offence I should therin commit a wrong. . . . I have no proofe
of evill wherwith to burthen her" (Cuniffe, II, 82). Yet, when
the news of the older sons' bad careers comes to his ears, he
does not hesitate to commit her to public humiliation.

To some extent, Gascoigne seems to be sympathetic to Lamia's
position. When the civil authorities are intent on prosecuting her,
he has Nuntius, a news carrier, say to Gnomaticus:

Nuntius: Good lord what a world is this? Justice quoth he? mary
    this is Justyce of the new fashion.
Gnomaticus: And what Justice good fellow I pray thee.
Nuntius: Nay none at all Sir, but rather an open wronge, an honest

old gentlewoman with her kinswoman are commaunded to the
coupe, onely because they suffered an honest youngman (and
Sonne to a welthy Burgher) to suppe with them yesternight, . . .
I have seldome heard of such rigor used, especially since they
proffer good suretyes to be always forth comming untill their
behaviour be tryed.   (Cunliffe, II, 70)

The women are not even to be allowed bail. But an additional
detail exposes the plight of Lamia. At the first suggestion of
trouble, her servingmen-protectors leave her to her fate .As
Eccho, the parasite, says earlier:

Tush *Dyck* hold thy peace, if we have not them, we shall have others
as good as they, thou mayst bee sure that as long as *Lamia* continueth
bewtifull, she shall never be without Sutors, and when the Crowes
feete groweth under her eye, why then no more adoe but ensineuate
thy selfe with another. Yea and in the meane time also, it should
be no bad councell, if a man had foure or five such hauntes in store,
that evermore when one house is on sweeping, another spytte may
cry creake at the fire: store is no sore as the proverbe saith, and
now adayes the broker which hath but one bargaine in hand, may
chaunce to weare a thred bare coate.   (Cunliffe, II, 66)

Finally, we learn that Lamia may even be in love with Phylosarchus, as Eccho again suggests: "Fye fie, what meaneth shee?
Will she cast away her selfe on this fashion for his sake? She
beareth but evill in remembraunce the good documentes of
that vertuous olde Lady her Aunte. I warrant you it would be
long before that *Messalina* would dye for love. Tush tush shall
I tell you? It is folly to stand meditation of these matters, every
man for himselfe and I for one..." (Cunliffe, II, 61). Lamia,
it seems, is caught in the snares of her youth. Being beautiful,
she is condemned as a temptress; being young, she is foolish
enough to fall in love, and sufficiently inexperienced to be used
by her Aunt, Eccho, and Dick Droome as their source of income.
Certainly, Lamia had few scruples, but Gascoigne gives us
more than just the surface portrait of a scheming woman. We
come to understand, through her, the barriers put in the way
of youth and the mortal danger waiting for those who trespass
across those barriers.

   If Lamia and the two elder brothers are not completely evil,
the results of their actions usually are. What, then, we must ask,
is it that turns young people into or allows them to become
criminals? The answer is highly ironic: their teachers! Gnomati-

cus and Pandarina, who are equally guilty for the tragedy of Lamia and the two elder brothers, are placed in obvious parallel positions early in the play. Gnomaticus delivers a sermon to the four youths in which, in elaborate and typically humanistic fashion, he instructs them to fear, love, and trust God: "I say, Feare God for he is might, love God, for he is mercifull, and trust in God for he is faithfull and just" (Cunliffe, II, 21). In the following scene, Pandarina counsels Lamia with almost parallel phrases, but of course with different intent: "I pray you learne these three pointes of me to governe your steppes by. First *Trust no man* how faire so ever he speake, next *Reject no man* (that hath ought) how evil favored so ever he be. And lastely *Love no man* longer than he geveth, since lyberall gyfts are the glewe of everduring love" (Cunliffe, II, 25). And Lamia replies in a tone of humility paralleling that of the four youths: "Well Aunt, I were worthy of great reprehension, if I would reject the good documents of such a frende, and if I have heretofore done contrary, impute it to my youth, but be you sure that hereafter I will endevour my selfe to follow your precepts" (Cunliffe, II, 25).

Pandarina gives Lamia evil counsel that is actually contrary to Lamia's nature (for she falls in love), and thus her counseling leads Lamia into the life of a criminal. Pandarina has some difficulty guiding Lamia, but society is ultimately on Pandarina's side, and, by the end of the play, it literally makes a hardened prostitute out of what at first was only a willful girl. Gnomaticus, on the other hand, aims at moral perfection for his four charges. The two parents retain him to instill the highest religious and civic ideals in their sons, and he virtually guarantees success. He chooses to teach four topics—their duty to God, to their king, to their country, and to their parents: His methods are to deliver sermons, to give them reading assignments, and to have them write poems and essays on the four subjects. His methods, in effect, are those of the humanist scholar-teacher. But Gnomaticus's major fault is that he does not understand human nature. He cannot recognize the signs of boredom and incipient rebellion in Phylautus and Phylosarchus, the two older sons; and he cannot, therefore, prevent their ruin. He believes in the essential goodness of the boys, and in this he is correct, for Phylosarchus, far from being a lustful seducer, wishes to write love poems to Lamia and to court her in a fairly conventional way.

But in his instruction, Gnomaticus relies too much on familiar proverbial wisdom and thereby disappoints the expectations of the elder brothers whose quick wits had already mastered this stage of education.

The content of instruction, as an exercise in abstraction and entirely without material relevant to the boys' daily lives, fails to satisfy the older brothers' desire for experience. So they search for it themselves, aided only by the corrupt servant, provided by Gnomaticus. Thus, both the humanistic education and the humanist educator fail to prevent the tragedy.

Another error, more directly fatal, is Gnomaticus's naïve trust of other human beings. Unable to recognize a corrupt servant, he trusts Ambidexter to watch over the four brothers at the university. Ambidexter, the bad servant, is directly responsible for leading the elder brothers to their ruin. Significantly, when the news of their disgrace and death is brought back, Gnomaticus is the first to receive it, perhaps because it is his failure more than anyone else's.

We found earlier that Gascoigne's early life somewhat followed the pattern of a prodigal son, so we must recognize that he understood their attitudes quite well. Perhaps this explains the absolute irreconcilability of the prodigals to society. Unlike other prodigal-son plays, neither the boys nor Lamia return to their parents' forgiving arms. Their parents certainly would take them, but somehow the real world does not operate so benevolently. Gascoigne, himself, although the son of a wealthy man, had to struggle for a living, and the experience left him without a neat formula for happiness and success, a point often made in his lyric poetry, such as "Gascoignes wodmanship." Thus, underneath the apparent respect he shows for Gnomaticus's teachings, there are notes of dislike for the two good sons. Their characters are flat and lifeless, they do their assigned tasks without question, and they often do more than is required in order to win Gnomaticus's approval. They frown upon their brothers' unconventionality, and in general show few human qualities, except when Phylotimus pleads to save Phylosarchus from a whipping. In one instance, when the two elder brothers have been rebuked by the Markgrave, the contrast in attitudes between the two sets of brothers is most marked:

Phylautus: Where have we bene quoth you? why we have bene with that good olde gentleman the Markgrave, unto whome

we were as welcome as water into the ship, the olde froward
frowner would scarce vouchsafe to speak unto us, or to looke
upon us, but he shall sit untill his heeles ake before I come
at him againe.

Phylomusus: O brother, use reverent speach of him, principally
bycause he is a Magistrate, and therwithal for his greye haires,
for that is one especiall poynt of our masters traditions.

Phylautus: Tushe what you tell me of our masters traditions? if a
Magistrate, or an elder would challendge reverence of a yong
gentleman, it were good reason also that they should render
affabilitie, and chearefull countenance to all such as present
them selves before them with good will. When we came to
him he knewe us not, ... (Cunliffe, II, 46)

This one incident illustrates one source of the conflict the elder
brothers have with society, the literal denial of equality to the
young by the elders; but it also summarizes the younger brothers
clearly. In effect, they represent all those whose success in life
springs from following a course laid out for them by others, from
obeying unquestioningly those in authority, and from maintain-
ing the traditional roles of society.

Gnomaticus, also, is given an unpleasant trait. When the
Nuntius tells him of Pandarina's and Lamia's arrest, he is not
even remotely concerned that they are held without the slightest bit of real evidence; even the Nuntius is astonished by this
lack of concern for justice. But, of course, Gnomaticus is worried
over his pupils, and the fate of someone on a lower social level
does not concern him.

Yet, despite the undercurrents of trouble, the play is designed
to depict humanistic concepts and techniques of education.
During the first two acts, Gnomaticus delivers lectures on duty
and morality and discusses concepts of philosophy with his four
pupils. Then he assigns them tasks in reading, in memorizing,
and in versifying. The view that poetry aids memory is voiced
by Gnomaticus: "and here I deliver the same unto you, to be
put in verse everie one by himself and in sundrie device, that
you may therein take the greater delight, for of all other Artes
Poetrie giveth greatest assistaunce unto memorie, since the verie
terminations and ceasures doe (as it were) serve for places
of memorie, and helpe the mynde with delight to carie burthens,
which else would seeme more grievous" (Cunliffe, II, 47-48).
The content of their study also is humanistic: they are to learn

154   GEORGE GASCOIGNE

their duties to God, king, country, and parents; and they are to learn how to express themselves well in rhetoric and poetry.

Another humanist attitude, one expressed by Queen Elizabeth's tutor Roger Ascham in *The Schoolmaster,* is that quick wits learn quickly but do not retain what they have learned, that they delight in pleasant studies but do not advance to more difficult labors, and that they usually come to a bad or inconsequential end. It seems almost that Ascham wrote the script, for the career followed by the two prodigals compares closely to his description of quick wits. The two prodigals have read extensively in the "pleasant" writings of Terence and Tully. They do the assigned work quickly and are bored by it, but they do not then apply themselves to more difficult material. Rather, they desire diversion and relaxation. And, of course, they come to a bad end.

Gnomaticus is aware of the quicker wits of the elder sons. When his servant praises their intellectual capacity: "and the two eldest could even then (in maner) record without booke as much as you had taught them," Gnomaticus replies: "Yea but what is that to the purpose? the quickest wits prove not alwayes best, for as they are readie to conceive, so do they quickly forget, & therewithall, the finenesse of their capacitie doth carie such oftentimes to delight in vanities, since mans nature is such, that with ease it inclyneth to pleasure, and unwilling it is to indure pain or travell, without the which no vertue is obteyned" (Cunliffe, II, 38). The conservative, less active, and less volatile mind was the preferred one; for it was less rebellious, less likely to stir up civil discord or religious doubts. It is difficult to take Gnomaticus's view on quick wits seriously, for it condemns his own teaching. Yet, the entire play is an exemplum of his and Ascham's view; and, in this respect, the prodigal-son story becomes really the one about rebels against traditional education. Education, after all, is the main perpetuating device of a culture or society; and one who rejects it is, in the eyes of that society, necessarily dangerous and must be either reclaimed or broken. In *The Glasse of Governement,* the two who choose to follow their own courses rather than those laid down by society are broken.

As I mentioned earlier, Gascoigne himself suffered the effects of prodigality. As a result, his attitude toward Phylosarchus and Phylautus is mixed. He sympathizes with their dilemma, but he feels forced to uphold the standards of his society. The subsequent conflict resulted in certain touches of character—to Lamia, to Gnomaticus, and to the two prodigals—which give the play strength and reality.

CHAPTER 9

Conclusion

GASCOIGNE'S contributions to literary history have been summarized repeatedly by scholars, and I have pointed to them in the appropriate sections of this book. In the different literary forms he worked with, he shows both technical facility and an experimental bent of mind; but, unfortunately, critics have overemphasized the experimental aspect and have neglected the intrinsic literary value of his work. Certainly, in assessing his "Certayne notes of Instruction," the contribution to literary history outweighs artistic considerations; through this work we are given an insight into the rules of thumb of contemporary poets and into the ideas on language held by one particular poetic mind. Its relative strangeness on the literary scene is emphasized by the way in which Gascoigne tried to disguise it by making it a letter of instruction to a friend rather than a public treatise of practical criticism. His mind, perhaps, but not his art is on display here.

I *Prose Fiction*

With respect to *The Adventures of Master F. J.*, his position is different. Here, Gascoigne is the creative experimenter, the leader of his time as a writer of prose fiction. The contemporary fiction varied from teaching moral lessons by means of historical or other examples to entertaining by the use of scenes of horror, of torture, and of depravity; but Gascoigne did not concern himself with any of these. In *The Adventures*, characterization is the primary interest; there is very little heavy moralizing in the story; and the lurid scenes are so filled with the ridiculous that they lose all resemblance to the more popular Italian *novelli*. Gascoigne used the story as a vehicle for satire, and he experimented with several methods of narration and presentation, using poems, an allegory, court-of-love debates, letters, and other devices. Unfortunately, English prose fiction took another

156

century to awaken; and *The Adventures,* buried behind the Renaissance, had little influence when it did. Many of the experiments Gascoigne made were made again by others—the judicious editor as narrator, the use of a short allegory, letters as a narrative device. To modern readers, *The Adventures* is still an enjoyable story; although the point of some of its satire is out of date, its wit and keen character perception keep it fresh and entertaining. To modern scholars, the work remains a puzzle because we wonder where such sophistication in prose fiction had its source. *The Adventures* is a monument of a sort, not to sixteenth-century prose fiction, but to its author who created a work of art which, in the complexity and originality of its construction, is out of context with its time.

II *Drama*

In the drama, Gascoigne's contributions to literary history are easily recognized. He brought contemporary Italian comedy to the stage, introducing nonpoetic dialogue with it; and he was also instrumental in the first production of a Greek tragedy. Unquestionably, his plays at Gray's Inn exerted considerable influence on the drama. However, the little-known *Glasse of Governement* has affected drama in a subtler way. Using the prodigal-son formula, it probed the conflicts between society's accepted values and the desires of characters whose abilities transcend the norm of society. The play showed the dramatic qualities inherent in this formula; and, although indirect, it is partly responsible for such plays as Shakespeare's *All's Well That Ends Well* and Marlowe's *Doctor Faustus,* plays in which the capable protagonist disregards society's laws and persuasions to make his own decisions about right and wrong, but who eventually is either welcomed back or destroyed. Gascoigne's play is antecedent to them. The conflict between the individual and his society became one of the major themes of the High Rennaissance; and Gascoigne, at the height of his career, was one of the first to give this conflict dramatic form.

III *Poetry*

Gascoigne is read more often as a critic or dramatist than as a poet, but his poetry occupies the bulk of his work and was the means by which he hoped to attain favor at court. He thought of himself primarily as a poet, and he recorded his most personal feelings, ideas, and criticism in his poems. In one sense, this self-expression hurt his chances for success; for his earlier poetry attempts to model itself after the Petrarchan, but his individual, often blunt expression missed the purpose of that graceful formula poetry. What comes through to us in all of his poems is his strong, individual voice—sardonic, sad, cynical, philosophical. On nearly every poem he wrote, Gascoigne left an individual mark that is as recognizable as a good painter's is in his painting. Gascoigne's strong personality, hard wit, and wry humor make his poems important; and these characteristics stem from his philosophy of language, from his patriotism, and from his belief that poetry, besides providing sensual pleasure for the reader, must reflect the author, his feelings about and attitudes toward the subject of the poem. Gascoigne described his own lusts and frustrations and triumphs, his own bitter recognition of failure and of approaching old age. The result is lyric poetry very closely linked to both Wyatt and Donne—poetry concerned with re-creating real experience in a masculine, English style. It does not focus on verbal decoration nor is it involved in the evolution of a standard imagery. It is concerned with metaphor and allegory, and it uses the directness and rhythm of colloquial speech to give it vitality and character.

Gascoigne's poetry is most important in that it strengthens and develops the native English tradition. In a period when poets were strongly drawn into the garden of Classical mythology and toyed with its golden fruit, Wyatt, Gascoigne, Donne, and a few others were still treading English soil and singing in unaccented voices. Under such lines as these from Gascoigne's "Philomene"

> In sweet April, the messenger to May,
> When hoonie drops do melt in golden showres,
> When every byrde records hir lovers lay,
> And westerne windes do foster forth our floures, . . .

we can feel the strength of Chaucer and the early balladeers. In Gascoigne's satiric and philosophical poetry, again, we feel the force of medieval English traditions. Yet, these older English traditions were close to being smothered by the weight of Classical and contemporary European poetry entering England. Without the experiments worked upon them by Wyatt, Gascoigne, and several others—the adaptation of the satire to the changing social environment, the dampening of strict moral and ethical dogma, the reworking of monotonous rhythms, the working of idiomatic and colloquial speech patterns into rigorous metrical units—much of the strength, beauty, and sense of purpose of the early English poetic tradition would have been extinguished by 1600. Wyatt, Gascoigne, Raleigh, Donne—by putting their own sure, ironic voices into their poetry, by making poetry reflect honestly their own emotions and attitudes—secured the continuance of the older English poetic tradition. Gascoigne's work led directly to development in High Renaissance drama and poetry; its importance is difficult to overestimate. However, as a creative artist, Gascoigne was able to put the observations, experience, and attitudes of a perceptive and individual Englishman into forms which endure through their own vitality and beauty and not just because of their usefulness as milestones in literary history.

Notes and References

Chapter One

1. The best biography of Gascoigne is C. T. Prouty, *George Gascoigne, Courtier, Soldier, and Poet* (New York, Columbia University Press, 1942). Useful are F. Schelling, *The Life and Writings of George Gascoigne,* University of Pennsylvania Series in Philology, Literature, and Archaeology, IV, No. 4; C. T. Prouty, "Gascoigne in the Low Countries and the Publication of A Hundred Sundry Flowers," *Review of English Studies,* XII (1926); and Genevieve Oldfield, "New Light on the Life of George Gascoigne," *Review of English Studies,* XIII (1937).

Chapter Two

1. Padelford discusses this point in the introduction to *Early Sixteenth Century Lyrics* (Boston, 1907).

2. Muir, *The Collected Poems of Sir Thomas Wyatt* (Cambridge: Harvard University Press, 1950), p. xxx.

3. Muir, in his work on Wyatt, says that "His finest poems are not, so far as we know, translations" (Introduction, p. xviii), and the reason he gives lies with the metrical difficulties. Further on, he says, "None of the sonnets, not even the late ones which are comparatively smooth, can be ranked among Wyatt's best poems" (Introduction, p. xxi).

4. Muir, p. 21.

5. Padelford, p. 34.

6. *Tottel's Miscellany,* ed. by Hyder Rollins (Cambridge: Harvard University Press, 1928), Vol. I, p. 169.

7. *Francesco Petrarca, Sonnets and Songs,* trans. by A. Armi (New York: Grosset and Dunlap, 1946), p. 249.

8. *Ibid.,* p. 253.

9. *Ibid.,* p. 257.

10. *Ibid.,* p. 411.

11. As pointed out by Thomas Baldwin in *On the Literary Genetics of Shakespeare's Poems and Sonnets* (Urbana: University of Illinois Press, 1950), this theme more properly was taken from Book 15 of Ovid's *Metamorphoses.* See Chapter 9, especially p. 276.

12. Armi, p. 419.

13. *Ibid.,* p. 459.

14. *Ibid.*, p. 159.
15. *Ibid.*, p. 127.
16. *Ibid.*, p. 385.
17. *Ibid.*, p. 471.

Chapter Three

1. Lawrence Babb, *The Elizabethan Malady* (East Lansing: Michigan State College Press, 1951), p. 143.
2. He repeats this image more explicitly in the first song of *The Grief of Joye*:

> I see not I: whereof yong men should bost,
> Since hee that is, nor fonde nor madd owtright,
> Dothe knowe y^t adge, will come at last like frost
> And nipp the flowers. . . .   (Cunliffe, II, 520)

Chapter Four

1. *The Poems of George Chapman*, ed. by Phyllis Bartlett (New York: Russell and Russell, 1941), p. 112.
2. *Ibid.*, pp. 112-13.
3. *Ibid.*, pp. 129-30.

Chapter Six

1. *History of English Poetry*, ed. by W. C. Hazlitt (London, 1871), Vol. IV, p. 364.
2. *Ibid.*, Vol. III, p. 234.
3. H. Walker, *English Satire and Satirists* (London, 1925), p. 63.
4. Alvin Kernan, *The Cankred Muse* (New Haven: Yale University Press, 1949), p. 41.
5. C. T. Prouty, *George Gascoigne, Elizabethan Courtier, Soldier, and Poet* (New York, Columbia University Press, 1942), p. 251.
6. Part of a slighting reference to *The Steele Glas* by R. Alden in his *The Rise of Formal Satire in England*, University of Pennsylvania Series in Philology, Archaeology, and Literature, VII, No. 2 (1899), p. 72.
7. *The Mirror for Magistrates*, ed. by Lily Campbell (Cambridge: at the University Press, 1938), p. 55.
8. Kernan, p. 49.
9. Prouty, p. 242.
10. A poisoned soap.
11. For a discussion of the character of Piers Plowman and his influence on sixteenth-century satire, see Kernan, pp. 43ff.

Chapter Seven

1. The most lucid discussion of the bibliographical problems of *The Adventures* is to be found in Prouty, *George Gascoigne*, particularly in Chapter VII.

2. See also Robt. Adams, "Gascoigne's 'Master F. J.' as Original Fiction," *Publications of the Modern Language Association*, LXXIII (1958), 315-26; Leicester Bradner, "The First English Novel, a Study of George Gascoigne's Adventures of Master F. J.," *Publications of the Modern Language Association*, XLV (1930); Richard Lanham, "Narrative Structure in Gascoigne's F. J.," *Studies in Short Fiction*, IV (1966), 42-50; and Charles W. Smith, "Structure and Thematic Unity in Gascoigne's F. J.," *Papers in Language and Literature*, II, 99-108.

3. For discussions of the courtly love traditions see W. G. Dodd, *Courtly Love in Chaucer and Gower* (Boston: Harvard Studies in English, Vol. I, 1913), and C. S. Lewis, *The Allegory of Love* (Oxford University Press, 1938).

Chapter Eight

1. See especially F. S. Boas, *University Drama in the Tudor Age* (Oxford: Clarendon Press, 1914); J. Cunliffe, *The Influence of Seneca on Elizabethan Tragedy* (London: Macmillan and Company, 1893); and F. L. Lucas, *Seneca and Elizabethan Tragedy* (Cambridge, at the University Press, 1922).

2. The most useful study of this type of play is C. H. Herford, *Studies in the Literary Relations of England and Germany in the Sixteenth Century* (Cambridge: at the University Press, 1886).

Selected Bibliography

PRIMARY SOURCES (*modern editions only*)

The Complete Works of George Gascoigne. 2 vols. John Cunliffe, editor. Cambridge, 1910.

"George Gascoigne's *A Hundreth Sundry Flowres*," C. T. Prouty, editor. *The University of Missouri Studies*, XVII, 2, 1942.

SECONDARY SOURCES

ADAMS, ROBERT P. "Gascoigne's 'Master F. J.' as Original Fiction." *Publications Modern Language Association*, LXXIII (1958), 315-26. Adams gives a well-documented and well-argued case for reading *Master F. J.* as original, imaginative fiction rather than as disguised autobiography.

BRADNER, LEICESTER. "Point of View in George Gascoigne's Fiction." *Studies in Short Fiction*, III (1965), 16-22. He discusses the differing roles of the narrator in "Dan Bartholomew of Bath" and the two versions of *Master F. J.*, showing the superior technique used in the earlier *F. J.* version.

HERFORD, C. H. *Studies in the Literary Relations of England and Germany in the Sixteenth Century*. Cambridge, 1886. He treats the subject of "school-drama" and the possible Latin and Continental models for Gascoigne's *Classe of Governement*.

ING, ELIZABETH. *Elizabethan Lyrics*. London, 1951. She gives a lucid discussion of Renaissance metrical theories and pays some rather ambivalent attention to Gascoigne's ideas on metrics found in his "Certayne notes of Instruction." She concludes that he is confused but occasionally perceptive.

KERNAN, ALVIN. *The Cankered Muse*. New Haven, 1949. He gives an intelligent survey of sixteenth-century satire but pays little attention to Gascoigne. He creates a perspective from which we can see Gascoigne's work clearly.

LANHAM, RICHARD. "Narrative Structure in Gascoigne's *F. J.*" *Studies in Short Fiction*, IV (1966), 42-50. He discusses the relationship to theme and structure of the two long "questions of love" in *F. J.*

OLDFIELD, GENEVIEVE. "New Light on the Life of George Gascoigne." *Review of English Studies*, XIII (1937), 129-38. One of the

best of the discussions of Gascoigne's marriage and his disinheritance.

PROUTY, C. T. "Gascoigne in the Low Countries and the Publication
of A Hundred Sundry Flowres." *Review of English Studies,* XII
(1936), 139-46. He compares the historical data with internal
poetic evidence in a discussion of the publication date of *A
Hundred Sundry Flowres.* His book, *George Gascoigne, Elizabethan Courtier, Soldier, Poet* (New York, 1942), is by far
the best discussion of Gascoigne's total career and its relation
to his poetry.

SCHELLING, F. *The Life and Writings of George Gascoigne.* University of Pennsylvania Series in Philology, Literature, and Archaeology, IV, 4. His discussion of the career and individual works
of Gascoigne have a more scholarly than a critical bent. He
attempts to piece together a coherent picture of Gascoigne's life.

WARD, B. M. "George Gascoigne and His Circle." *Review of English
Studies,* II (1926), 32-41. He quotes from legal documents
such as Gascoigne's father's will and William Breton's will to
show Gascoigne's relationship with his own family and with
his in-laws.

WINTERS, YVOR. "The Sixteenth Century Lyric: Part I," *Poetry,* LIII
(February 5, 1939), 258-72, and "The Sixteenth Century Lyric:
Part II," *Poetry,* LIII (March 6, 1939), 320-35. Winters separates the Petrarchan poetry of the sixteenth century from the
aphoristic and expository poetry, and he concludes that Gascoigne not only is the best poet in the aphoristic school but is
one of the best six or seven lyric poets of his age.

Index

(The works of Gascoigne are listed under his name.)

165